# Paul P. Ashley

# You and Your Will

## THE PLANNING AND MANAGEMENT OF YOUR ESTATE

## Revised Edition

G.K.HALL & CO.

 Boston, Massachusetts

1977

Library of Congress Cataloging in Publication Data

Ashley, Paul Pritchard, 1896-
  You and your will.

  Large print ed.
  Includes index.
  1.  Wills—United States—Popular works.
  2.  Estate planning—United States— Popular works.
  I.  Title.
  [KF755.Z9A48  1976]   346'.73'054  76-27720
  ISBN 0-8161-6420-7

Published in Large Print by arrangement with McGraw-Hill Book Company

Set in Photon 18 pt Crown

*To Katherine*

# Contents

# You
# and
# Your
# Will

# Preface

This book is designed to prepare the client to make maximum and economical use of an attorney and any other advisers consulted incident to planning an estate. Its purpose is to furnish a testator with background for the writing of a wiser will and for effective administration.

When does a well-drawn will, perhaps preceded by *inter vivos* gifts, become important? At what level of affluence? Whatever a family owns is its financial universe. Often it is more difficult to allocate a modest estate than a large one. In the latter case, there is enough for all. In the former, the parent may be hard-pressed to safeguard the spastic child without diverting needed educational funds from the son who yearns to become an astrophysicist or from the daughter with great musical talent. Herein will be a few suggestions in respect to stretching the dollars.

And in a decade or two or more when death taps at the door, your estate may be far larger than you now envisage. It may be so already. One tends to think in terms of a few principal segments of one's estate. For purposes of planning, your "estate" includes everything of monetary value: your home and other real estate; all bank and savings accounts; usables including *objets d'art* and hobbies, such as a stamp collection; your carefully planned investment portfolio; life insurance; rights under a pension plan, if you enjoy that umbrella; as well as growing protection from social security. All must be arranged so as to afford maximum benefit to the beneficiaries.

This is not a do-it-yourself manual. A wrongly drawn or improperly executed will may spell disaster for loved ones — litigation, undesired results, unnecessary taxes, and other evils. Wills are important documents and should be treated with due respect.

Relatively few lawyers will be interested in this book. For those already skilled in planning and drafting wills and, importantly, in the actual administration of estates, it tells nothing new. For those who expect to become proficient, it would be but a beginning — they want far more. The 1961 edition of a text on estate planning, written for lawyers, was published in two volumes: 1,750 pages. The 1972 edition reaches 2,415 pages.

Able trust officers, accountants, and life insurance underwriters have specialized skills. All, from their own viewpoints, may have much to contribute to the planning of the large or involved estate.

The subject of wills and the administration of estates calls for more than the lightest of reading. However, technical words are usually defined when first used: *inter vivos,* used just a little earlier, means during one's lifetime. A glossary follows Chapter 14 for your convenience when the meaning of a term proves elusive.

Wherever the work "testator" is used, it is to mean either man or woman unless the context demands a different meaning. In many other instances, the ancient legal habit of using the male to include the female may be followed. And, for example, the term "bank" embraces "trust company"; the singular includes the plural, and vice versa, unless the context demands otherwise. The words "testator" (he or she who draws the will) and "you" are used interchangeably.

For reading and commenting upon an almost-final draft of the entire manuscript, I owe a debt of gratitude to James Cherry, Esq., of the New York Bar and to Loren E. Juhl, Esq., of the Chicago Bar, both eminent in the fields of estate planning and taxation; and also to L. L. Allison, veteran trust officer with territorial jurisdiction from Seattle to San Diego. I followed most of their suggestions, but not all of them. So whether of omission or commission, errors are mine alone.

*Paul P. Ashley*

# ONE

# Wills

A will is a wondrous thing. It confers a modicum of immortality. For many years after death, a person who makes a will may direct the management and distribution of his or her property from beyond the grave.

How is a will defined? In 1769, a Society of Gentlemen in Scotland began publication of a work then and still called the *Encyclopaedia Britannica*. The first edition says that "will"

signifies the declaration of a man's mind and interest relating to the disposition of his lands, goods, or other estate, or of what he would have done after his death.

The law has developed mechanisms for doing what the makers of wills say they themselves would have done.

This right or privilege to direct disposition of property is not now unlimited, nor has it ever been. Under Roman jurisprudence it was not enjoyed by all, as it is today under Anglo-American law. During the Dark Ages and the feudal days which followed, this prerogative was almost nonexistent for ordinary people. It has varied throughout the centuries and now differs according to the law of the land.

Most jurisdictions overrule a testator who attempts to will all away from the spouse. Children must not be forgotten; some statutes provide that they must be accorded an allotted portion. A bequest may not be conditioned upon an act repulsive to society. In some states the court will refuse to enforce, or may modify, a will which shocks the conscience of the judge.

Unless dedicated to charitable purposes, the property of testator cannot be tied up indefinitely — the rule against perpetuities. The usual formula is that the trust property must vest (belong absolutely to someone) not later than the death of the longest-lived beneficiary in being at the time of testator's death plus twenty-one years plus such periods of gestation as in fact exist. When the will includes multiple small children as beneficiaries, this may be a long time.

Whenever possible, estate planning should be a project of both husband and wife, with children brought in on some of the discussions as early as is suitable. Yet, often parents do not permit adult, steady children to participate in planning their own financial futures. Sometimes a will is kept a deep, dark secret — or even used as a veiled threat. Except in extreme circumstances, that is malefic. Nevertheless, there are situations where the will is an intensely personal affair; good reasons may exist why, for example, the husband should not be told what the wife has written.

The ultimate test of a will is — does it seem basically right and fair? If the answer is "No," it is not the best will possible. Or at least it is not worded in a manner which best conveys testator's kindly and sagacious intent. A mother who owns but one really valuable jewel might say:

I bequeath my five-carat diamond ring to my daughter Kathy, and my garnet earrings to my daughter Sue.

Perhaps to Sue and the cousins it would seem quite different if the mother had directed:

I bequeath my diamond ring to my older daughter Kathy, unless she should predecease me. Then of course it will go to my daughter Sue, unto whom I also bequeath all the rest of my jewelry. If Sue should predecease me, all the jewelry shall pass to Kathy.

This is but an example. Here and there throughout this book, mention will be made of the desirability of a few words which reveal a testator who is thoughtful and sympathetic rather than arbitrary and capricious.

Certainly taxes should be minimized, both death dues (duties) and those measured by income. How to do so is the subject of Chapters 12 and 13. But your primary concern is accomplishing *what you deem best* for those to whom you owe a duty and, indeed, for all the beneficiaries of your bounty. Only then does your will give peace of mind.

## FORMALITIES

Following the grand traditions of France, in Louisiana the execution of a will is a ceremony. Every state demands certain formalities. That is as it should be. When a document is produced and offered as a will, the person who signed it cannot be present to testify as to whether or not he or she intended it *as a will*. If alive, the individual might have testified:

Yes, that is my signature. I doubtless signed it along with a number of other papers. Often I see no more than the final page. I cannot reread, even read, everything.

I signed the last page of this four-page instrument, but no one mentioned it pretends to be a new will. I certainly did not intend it as such.

But this person's lips are now sealed by death. Or perhaps a deceased wife, if able to testify, would have said she always signed the papers her husband brought home for her signature. He never spoke of a will.

No, the alleged testator, now dead, cannot personally correct a mistake or thwart a fraud. Hence, everywhere the law has strict requirements in respect to the execution of wills. They vary somewhat from state to state. In most states, two witnesses are required; presently in some states, three. A notary public is not a substitute for witnesses.

At time of the execution, testator must declare the document to be a will and must personally request the witnesses to attest the signature. They must then do so, substantially in the form required in that state. The mandate may be that they must sign in the presence of the testator and in the presence of one another, and the testator in theirs.

Though legally unnecessary, it is good practice for testator to sign or initial every every page, in ink. Then sheets cannot be substituted.

The will must be executed according to the laws of the jurisdiction (the state) wherein it is subscribed. If so executed in good faith, as far as the formalities are concerned, it will be valid anywhere. Nevertheless, a testator making a new will while away from home — that is, when outside the state of permanent residence where, presumably, the probate proceedings will occur — would be prudent, promptly upon return, to revitalize the document by execution before local witnesses under the guidance of the testator's accustomed counsel. Incidentally, securing the testimony of distant witnesses by deposition may cause delays and involve unnecessary expense. Local witnesses often testify without charge.

## Witnesses

The usual witness does not read any of the will. Witnesses need only be able to testify that testator signed the will in their presence, declared it to be maker's last will and testament, and requested the required witness or witnesses to attest the execution of the document as a will, and that they did so.

The ideal person is a stable adult who knows testator and, if testator is venerable, is younger than that individual. Even then, the witness may die first or be unavailable when the time comes to testify. It may be convenient if his or her signature can be readily verfied, as can that of a lawyer whose name appears on many court papers, of a doctor whose illegible scrawl can be confirmed by a pharmacist and 10,000 prescriptions, or of some other suitable person whose signature can be proved easily.

Persons interested in the estate, whether directly or indirectly, should not be witnesses. This group includes beneficiaries, heirs, executors, and trustees, and their spouses. An officer or the principal stockholders of a corporate beneficiary might be challenged.

Itinerants, whether of high or low degree, are not desirable witnesses. They may not be handy when needed. Sick in his hotel room, one testator executed his will before two bellhops as witnesses. He named a major bank as executor-trustee, but did not bother to tell the trust officers about it. Four years later, he died without having made a new will as he had been admonished to do. Neither bellhop could be located. The proving of testator's signature was difficult and expensive. Had the uniforms been those of admirals, the witnesses would have been findable, but perhaps reachable only after frustrating delays.

If there can be the slightest question as to testator's mental capacity, the witnesses should be chosen with that risk in mind — the physicians, nurses, or other persons who can, if necessary, sustain their conviction that testator had the requisite mental ability.

When the will of Katheryn Koman was presented for probate, it was resisted on the ground that it had not been actually executed by her. She was too weak to use a pen. The scrivener held her hand to the pen and guided it without her having expressly authorized him to do so. In 1970 the Supreme Court of Wisconsin decided that this was insufficient to constitute execution of a valid will by Mrs. Koman. The judges thus overruled a 1934 Wisconsin decision involving the will of Walter Wilcox, which held that physical touching of the pen by testator while the signature is affixed is the sole requirement for a proper execution.

These two decisions well illustrate the conservative care which should be exercised whenever there is a question as to the mental or physical condition of the testator. When attendant upon the execution of her will, Mrs. Koman's lawyer may have been relying on the decision in the Wilcox case, thirty-five years earlier.

# HOLOGRAPHIC WILLS

The holograph is an emergency exception to execution of a will with customary rites. A holographic will must be written entirely by the hand of the person who signs it. Repeat *entirely;* a partially printed date such as "197 — ," filled in by testator, may void it. It is a gamble. In some of these fifty United States, it is not valid.

The use of a holograph may be justified by military personnel on active duty or by sailors at sea. But when home from the wars or safe again on shore, the maker of the holographic will should promptly formulate and execute another with usual formalities and witnesses.

# WHO CAN MAKE A VALID WILL?

Testamentary capacity means mental ability of any man or woman sufficient for the making of a will. The testator must be able to understand the nature of the document and the consequence of signing it. Factors bearing on that modest test of capacity include: (1) Does testator seem to know what a will is? (2) Does the person have a fair idea of what is now owned or may be owned before death comes? (3) Does the individual remember at least some people toward whom most testators would feel a duty? (4) Is testator "of unsound mind" in the sense of having significant delusions?

The testator need not be good at business or adept in planning for the disposal of property. In fact, the person may be stupid or unfair. Yet the will will stand, unless fraud or undue influence has been imposed upon its maker's inadequacy.

Famed Commodore Cornelius Vanderbilt built his railroad fortune to an estate worth in the order of $100,000,000 in 1877 money. He left a second wife, eight daughters, and two sons. He believed that death had not terminated communication with his beloved first wife, Sophie. Mediums arranged séances.

Upon the advice of Sophie, he left most of his fortune to their son William. The remainder went to the second wife and, unequally, to the nine other children. In view of the visions upon which the Commodore had, at least in part, relied, some of the children contested the will. The trial judge admitted the document to probate. Belief in messages from the dead did not destroy the competency of the Commodore to execute a valid will.

Not long ago, a Kentucky colonel died at the age of seventy-seven, leaving eight children and several grandchildren. He was very emotional. Because of arthritis and arteriosclerosis, he was biologically five or six years older than his chronological age. Two years before his death, a son took him to that son's lawyer. A will was executed, leaving the entire estate to this son, who kept the will in his own box and saw to it that the father was never alone with the other children. When the will was offered for probate, they contested it. The court upheld them. Relatively slight evidence of undue influence or lack of mental capacity may invalidate the will if coupled with a showing of an unnatural division of testator's property.

Age requirements differ and occasionally change as state legislatures convene. They range from the conventional "anyone over twenty-one years" down to (in one state only) fourteen. Three states believe that marriage shows wisdom and attribute testamentary capacity to any married person. Another state limits that happy assumption to women. Members of the Armed Forces and, in at least one state, sailors in the Merchant Marine enjoy special status. Some states make an age distinction between those willing real estate and those willing personal property (movables, including intangibles, such as stocks and bonds).

So, in respect to age, the summation must be: If you are under twenty-one, find out.

And if anyone below the age of twenty-one should execute a will in a state with a requirement below three times seven, expecting it to be valid in a state which does require twenty-one years, testator should secure the opinion of counsel in the twenty-one-year state. Similarly, real estate situated in a twenty-one-year state will not ordinarily pass under a will executed by a younger person, even though such disposition would be valid in the state where the will was signed.

Physical handicaps do not abrogate testamentary capacity. With proper formalities, and with the will being read aloud, a blind person may execute a will. With appropriately different rituals, so may a person who is deaf or dumb. A testator unable to read or write may sign an "X" if the document is then read aloud and attested in accordance with the law of the jurisdiction where executed. All special situations must be handled with exquisite care.

## WHERE LODGE YOUR WILL?

For those who have a safe-deposit box within the steel walls of a bank or other public vault, the question, "Where shall I keep my will?" would seem to call for an easy and unequivocal response: "There." Unfortunately, in a number of states, this is not the wise thing to do.

Sometimes compelled by law and sometimes by custom, after your death the institution which operates the vaults will not permit access except by a delegate appointed by the court, accompanied by a representative of the state taxing authority. That restriction necessitates the expense of an unnecessary court maneuver. There might be a harmful delay over a three-day weekend.

Or there may be postponements if it is impossible to synchronize the schedules of the taxgatherer, your attorney, and the court's appointee.

In states which maintain such roadbocks, whether by statutory mandate or because of custom, most attorneys will advise against sequestering the will in a box which may be unavailable the very day and hour your executor needs desperately to open it.

In other states, your box at the bank may be the ideal place. Your safe deposit contract may authorize entrance by two or more persons, the death of one not affecting the right of another to enter.

The form now before me has lines for four signatures. Spaces for identifying data for each of the four signers (birthday, birthplace, color of eyes, height, weight, references, mother's maiden name) are available on the reverse side of the safe deposit contract. In short, each of those authorized to enter the box is self-sufficient. And so it is that *if* you reside in an informal state and *if* there are two or three persons, or even one, who during your lifetime have access to your box, it is a natural place to cache your will.

But where should you store your will if you live in a strict state? Now and then, vault keepers say, husband and wife separately rent two boxes, his will in hers and her will in his. This does not solve a common accident.

Where outside of boxes? Not hidden under the shirts in your bureau drawer or even in your file in your home library. Not in the secret drawer in the antique desk you inherited from Uncle Archie; perhaps no one will be able to find it. If it is to be at home, remember that fire, not theft, is the great destroyer. Vandals want TV sets and silver rather than dreary-looking documents.

Not in your personal file at the office unless you are in a Class A fireproof building and your own filing cabinet is fire-resistant. Perhaps your attorney has a truly fireproof safe; if so, that should be a relatively safe place. But if you leave it there, by all means have a completely conformed copy in your own safest spot. By "conformed copy" is meant one with all the blanks filled in, just as on the original. Boldly marked "Copy," a Xerox is suitable for this purpose. Perhaps you are one of the rare persons who has an actually fireproof home safe.

Testators inquire about having a duplicate signed original. There are persuasive points against that practice. Two examples: The testator might revoke the one in his or her box by destroying it. The duplicate original, available because stored elsewhere, might be presented for probate as a valid original will, though testator thought it had been revoked. Or, if the will recites that it was executed in duplicate and if one counterpart cannot be found, should the probate judge assume that it was destroyed by testator, thus revoking the will?

If you have named a bank as executor, it will be a natural custodian unless you think that you may change executors and do not want the embarrassment of telling the bank (from which you borrow) that it no longer is your executor.

## TYPICAL CONTENTS

Below, in briefest and general terms, is listed the range of provisions which will be found in typical wills of well-situated testators.

1. *Identification of testator.* Meticulous spelling of full name: "I, Charleston Zane Boyd commonly known as and who sometimes appears of record as Charlie Z. Boyd or Charley Boyd."

2. *Declaration* that this document is Boyd's last will and testament; *revocation* of all former wills and codicils. (A codicil is a supplement

19

which adds to, deletes from, or modifies the provisions of a will.)

3. If complicated, *nature of property* briefly described. Where the records are which will show what belongs to testator, what belongs to the spouse separately, and what is joint or community property (see Glossary) In a community property state,* the assumption may be that all is community. The postmortem segregation process should be facilitated.

4. *Names of all children,* including those by previous marriage. If there are illegitimate children, whether or not testator openly acknowledges them, he or she should ask the attorney's advice as to what should be said.

5. *Specific bequests and devises;* that is, legacies of particular things, tangible or intangible, real or personal, or fixed amounts of money that are singled out to go to a specified person

---

*Arizona, California, Idaho, Louisiana, Nevada, New Mexico, Texas, Washington.

or institution.

In the course of spelling out the specific allocations, testator should direct the line of succession, if any. "Mill Valley Farm to my son Scott, if he survives me. If Scott predeceases me but my nephew Edward survives me, the farm shall pass to Edward. If both predecease me, the farm becomes part of my residuary estate."

6. *Establishment of trusts,* if any. (The nature of trusts, living and testamentary, is pictured in Chapter 7. Meanwhile, scores of references are made to provisions of a will which become effective through the ancient legal invention called a trust, operated by a trustee. I am, as it were, telling where one can go in the automobile before describing what an automobile is. To me, that seems better than now diverting to talk about trusts as trusts. But to many readers, trust terms may be so unfamiliar that they will prefer to read about trusts generally, in Chapter 7, before proceeding much further.)

7. General powers of *trustees* and

special instructions to them.

8. *Dispositive provisions,* stating where income is to be channeled and when and where principal will eventually vest.

9. How *taxes* are to be allocated.

10. *Personal representative(s)* (executor) named and powers delineated.

11. The *attestation* clause in accordance with the law of the realm where executed. This clause appears after testator's signature. The witnesses attest that testator signed the document, declared it to be his or her will, and asked them to witness it.

Not all these provisions are reflected in every will. And other aspects could be listed. For example, it might be prudent to include particular provisions covering simultaneous (or nearly so) accidental deaths and deaths from any cause within, say, five months of each other. But the list is a fair schematic, as an architect might say, of what the completed plans will contain.

The law does not require scientific use of mystic words. If the meaning of the testator is understandable, it will be enforced unless unlawful.

## A MINIMUM WILL

In contrast, here follows, in full, a simple will valid in most jurisdictions. It is not recommended for anyone.

Provincetown, New Hampshire
August 13, 1879

I will everything which I possess to Priscilla whom I expect to marry tomorrow.

*Jonathan Trumbull*
Jonathan Trumbull

In presence of:

*Obediah Hodson*
Witness

*Elizabeth Leaden*
Witness

23

Jonathan's failure to name an executor is not serious. Priscilla is sole devisee. It is expectable that if they marry and her husband should die while this will is in effect, the court would appoint her administratrix with the will annexed, meaning that she is to carry out the terms of the will.

However, Jonathan's hasty home product does leave openings for litigation if they do not exchange vows as scheduled. Does the will mean all to Priscilla *if* Jonathan marries her as expected, or to her regardless? What if there is a lovers' quarrel and the wedding is postponed or canceled, with no one quite sure which? Jonathan dies during the third month, not having renounced the will. What then?

Or suppose Jonathan is killed by a fall from his horse en route home from the traditional bachelor dinner the boys put on a few hours after he signed the document. Should the fair Priscilla and her successors have the property — or should Jonathan's widowed mother?

# WHAT IF NO WILL?

When there is no will, it is called an intestacy. The machinery of the law takes over and commands how the estate shall be distributed. The probate judge may be among the most kindly of persons, anxious to do everything possible for the bereft family. But a judge must operate within the framework of impersonal law. The result may be gross unfairness, completely at variance with the wishes of decedent and the needs of those dependent upon the estate.

Though usually unnecessarily cumbersome and hence costly, the intestate procedures are not outrageous. In a small, uninvolved estate, required notices and court routines may be the only visible difference between an intestacy and administration of a similar modest estate under a will. The survivor, if a man, is called administrator rather than executor; or, if a woman, administratrix instead of executrix. As either administrator or administratrix, this person may be required to post a bond to assure honest performance, when as executor or executrix, the estate would be spared that additional expense. Perhaps as administratrix, for example, a wife must file petitions and secure court approval before doing sensible things with the property of the estate, when, as executrix, she could have done whatever a prudent person should do without bothering with a petition for authority, perhaps notices, and a court hearing. In a larger estate, the difference in cost of doing the many things which must be done may be considerable.

While in terms of dollars the intestacy may not be prohibitive, the distortion in the lives of the survivors may be tragic. Assume a young couple, Don and Gretchen, and two small children. Including their equity in their home and his life insurance, Don's gross estate was slightly over $53,000. On his death, the life insurance furnished sufficient cash to meet the expenses of Don's illness, pay the balance on the house, and cover current bills. Grandmother moved in to care for the children and Gretchen went back to her old job. There being no will, in that state one-half the property (about $25,000 in value) went to Gretchen and one-fourth (about $12,500) to each of the children.

The lawyer prepared papers asking the court to appoint Gretchen guardian of the property of her own children. A social service worker appeared from the woodwork and quizzed her. She was appointed. For twenty years as to the younger child and for eighteen as to the older, Gretchen, as guardian, must make periodic reports to the court. Perhaps she had to be bonded. The sale of the house necessitated another pilgrimage to court; how otherwise can the law protect minors and incompetents whose affairs are in the hands of third parties?

The little will described on page 35 as the First Will of the succession of wills discussed in the next chapter would have put everything in the hands of Gretchen, saving much needed money and avoiding travail.

This one somewhat detailed human

illustration must suffice, though a multitude could be given. Here follow a number of ultimate reasons why everyone who owns property should have a will.

## Legislatures decide divisions

The deceased having ignored the legal right to direct the disposition of the property, the law must surmise what intestate would have done. Legislative imaginations vary. Usually the surviving spouse will receive from one-third to one-half of the estate — not all, as is often supposed. The balance will go to children, or if there are none, to surviving parents, or even to brothers and sisters or more distant kin. Or the survivor must divide with the children, share and share alike. The beneficiaries are but percentages.

As illustrated with Don and Gretchen, the estate may be compartmentalized by guardianships. Sound overall management may be difficult or even impossible.

## Plans by testator

A will can give general and special orders for the handling of foreseeable situations. Testator can direct to be done (as said in the ancient definition) "what he would have done after his death." A testator can provide for minors, the aged, and the handicapped as she or he deems best within the limits of the estate. There can be a flexible fund to educate the children according to their needs and capabilities. If testator wants anything to go to siblings, the will can make distinctions between them. Variations are legion.

A will is a human document. In contrast, its substitute, the laws of descent and distribution, cannot be personalized. Fifty legislatures enact what they think the decedent should have wanted, a sort of data processing determination.

## Choose your own personal representative

Someone must manage your estate during the postmortem period. Shall this person be someone you appoint in your will? Or do you want to chance a total stranger appointed by a judge?

## Guardians of your loved ones

Statistically, I suppose, most court-chosen guardians are the very persons the decedent would have wished. Typically, a surviving father or mother. Indeed, by statute, a surviving parent may have a legal right to be appointed guardian of the child. But if both parents should go, they might not want the judge-chosen guardian as a result of an intestacy.

## Your investments

The law has machinery and appoints personnel for the long- as well as the short-range handling of your properties. But certainly the executors and trustees of your own choice can be expected to do a better job than the nominee of a judge, a semiqualified person perhaps unacquainted with either your family or its business affairs. Or the judge might appoint the very bank you would not have chosen!

## Taxes and costs

The impact of taxes and the cost of settling your estate can be reduced.

## Who writes the rules?

The ultimate distinction between a will and an intestacy is very simple. In essence, it is the person or agency that writes the rules. Is it you, the testator? Or the legislature and public officials?

The question — who writes the rules? applies to all manner of management matters as well as to the dispositive provisions. ''Dispositive'' provisions direct how your property will be distributed, to whom, and subject to what directions. Illustrations have already been given and many more will follow.

## THE PSYCHOLOGY OF MAKING A WILL

Not unnaturally and not infrequently, there is an internal resistance to the development and execution of a will. Many would-be testators simply cannot bring themselves to make decisions and instruct their scribes. There are repeated conferences on the same facet, punctuated with postponements. Unless testator feels under pressure (in anticipation of an operation or a flight to Burma), there may be an inexplicable lag between completion of the document and signing. I suppose the act of signing savors of preparing to die. The longest delay I have observed between completion of the final draft on bond paper and execution was four years. Then, without changing one jot or tittle of the aging draft, without even a telephone call, testator came in and signed it one day while I was in court.

One should have a positive attitude

toward the making of a will. It cares for loved ones. It anticipates their requirements. If well done, the will may, for many years, benefit the family, even descendants yet unborn.

Not forgetting that to sign a will hurriedly at the hospital just before surgery is no fun, I suggest that the drawing of the will be viewed as a normal constructive project — something testator is doing on behalf of those people and purposes which are nearest and dearest.

# TWO

# Changing Conditions — Evolving Wills

The writing is often entitled *Last Will and Testament*. Except in the relatively infrequent instances of a will signed *in extremis* (when the testator believes he or she is about to die), "last" is but a conventional word, like a useless button on a man's coat sleeve, put there by the lawyer who tailored the document. Obsolescence applies to wills as well as to things physical. "Last" really means no more than "until I make another," or "until I change this by a codicil."

# A SUCCESSION OF WILLS

A will is ambulatory. Unless frozen by a contract, as is sometimes wise to do, it is subject to change whenever the testator so desires. To illustrate a natural progression of wills, let us assume that a couple started the marital state with little more than a table of wedding presents. Over the years they accumulated a fortune. They executed six wills, averaging them about seven years apart. All were called "last."

*First Will:* All to each other or, in the event of the death of both of them, to their (then hoped-for) children, share and share alike. If they should both die without issue, to parents, or brothers and sisters. By "issue" is meant offspring: descendant or descendants.

*Second Will:* Three children have arrived. An instantaneous estate has been created by life insurance; a little has been saved and a little inherited. Still, all to each other. But in the event of the death of both, all to a trustee for the care of the children. Designation of a guardian by

35

codicil will be described in Chapter 6 (pages 134-35).

*Third Will:* The estate has been growing. One of the children is handicapped. Still, all to each other if one survives. In the event of the death of both, a trust which includes special provisions for protecting the disadvantaged child, augmented by a suitable additional insurance policy on the father's life. Guardian changed.

*Fourth Will:* The estate has become so large that taxes have become a factor. Husband needs freedom to use their capital in his growing business. Wife wants no avoidable business responsibilities. *Husband's Will:* Home and usables to wife. In a common law state, half the rest in a marital trust (see Glossary) and half in a residuary trust for benefit of wife and children. In a community property state, all of husband's half of investments to the residuary trust, the trust to which go all assets not ordered elsewhere. *Wife's Will:* All still to husband if he survives her. Availability of capital to husband, unrestricted by any trust, is believed more important than saving taxes. In trust if both should die. Very liberal provisions in respect to the disadvantaged child.

*Fifth Will:* The husband's business was recently sold to a conglomerate. Family investment assets now in a conservative portfolio. Husband is on salary, with a retirement plan. *Husband's Will:* In a common law state, husband's will creates a marital trust for benefit of wife and residuary trust for her benefit and that of the children, which protects the handicapped son. In a community property state, decedent husband's half is devised and bequeathed in trust for benefit of the survivor and the children. The size of the estate now justifies an appropriate distribution at designated ages to the two well children while mother still lives. The special trust for benefit of the handicapped son continues during his lifetime; upon his death, it will be distributed to his brother and sister or their issue. There will be a worthwhile saving in taxes.

*Sixth Will:* The handicapped son is gone. Now well into their seventies, with the approval of their son and daughter, these wealthy testators, now grandparents, (1) bequeath all usables and $100,000 each to their two children, and (2) place the rest in trust for grandchildren and potential great-grandchildren, with some tax savings in mind but primarily to stabilize the family.

## CODICILS

A new will need not be executed every time a change is indicated. Often a codicil will suffice — perhaps but one page. A codicil is a supplement adding to, deleting from, or modifying the terms of a will. Executed with the formalities of a will, it may be admitted to probate. It should carefully identify the will and previous codicils, if any there be, and affirm those portions it does not modify.

Codicils can be overdone. By the time the testator reaches the third codicil, ambiguities may arise. It is time to integrate the documents into one new will.

Kindness and good taste enter into the

writing of codicils. Suppose the will includes a number of specific bequests of money or things to relatives and close friends. Testator decides to delete one or two legacies, increase some, and decrease others. He or she believes there are good reasons for doing so. But unless the reasons are such that they can be reflected by a few words in the codicil, understandable by all concerned and acceptable to those deleted or downgraded, feelings may be sorely hurt. It is better to redo the entire will so that the changes will be known only to the testator and to the amanuensis.

Indeed, in some jurisdictions, when a codicil eliminates or reduces a legacy, the disadvantaged person must be given an opportunity to protest in court if she or he cares to do so. The person must be located and served with a notice, often called a citation. If you are considering a reduction in amount or value by *codicil,* it is prudent to ask counsel whether an aggrieved beneficiary would have a right to object.

A testator should never try to change

an existing will by erasures or interlineations. An interlineation *before* execution, properly initialed by the testator and witnesses, to show approval, is part of the will itself. But changes afterward are in the nature of codicils without being signed and witnessed with the required formalities. They are a fertile ground for trouble.

Circumstances continually change, often suddenly and dramatically, but sometimes so stealthily that testator does not note that an important variation has occurred. The legal necessity or practical desirability of an immediate codicil or a new will should have testator's attention upon happenings involving (1) *personal* change within the family or among principal beneficiaries — a birth, marriage, divorce, or death; (2) *property* — significant changes in value or nature; (3) *vocation* and *residence,* particularly if testator moves to a new state; (4) a *fiduciary* who becomes unable to serve or is outmoded. And through some channel you should be made aware of new laws, tax and other, affecting your estate.

## INTENTIONAL REVOCATION

Revocation of a present will should be incident to the execution of the new will. The preamble paragraph should always include ". . . and revoke all former wills and codicils by me made."

If a testator (possibly angry at a principal beneficiary) decides that, for a time at least, it would be preferable to die intestate and have the estate settled according to the fixed laws of descent and distribution, the successors may be saved much trouble if there is a clear record to the effect that the will was in fact revoked. Otherwise, there may be days or weeks of searching for a lost will and a long period of uncertainty. A lawyer's secretary may testify:

This is an unsigned carbon copy of the will I typed. The testator declared it to be his will. At his request, Mr. Barrister and I signed as witnesses, both of us in his presence. Testator took the original with him. Here on the carbon, in my writing, appears the notation "Original delivered to client."

Tearing or burning a will with the intent to revoke it is a recognized method of revocation. But, if done in solitude or in the presence of one witness who happens to predecease the revoker, whence comes the evidence of that dramatic act of revocation? The older son testifies:

I am certain Mother had a will. When she visited us at Christmas time she told me about it. Where could she have put it?

And the hunt continues. It may be difficult to prove to the court that the mother died intestate. A carbon of the will which the pseudotestator had carefully torn to bits might be offered for probate as her last will and testament and a contest ensues. The evidence *might* be such that the judge believes he has before him a carbon of a lost, but existing, valid will.

The point is that if a will is to be

revoked without a simultaneous replacement, there should be a paper where the will itself would have been, affirming the revocation or, as the saying goes, the burning should be in the presence of twenty bishops.

Cancellation across the face of the will signed by the testator, obliteration, erasures, and other clumsy methods may or may not be effective. They invite litigation. But an unequivocal holographic revocation will be recognized as effective in a state which recognizes holographic wills.

No space is spent here on partial revocation because, I hope, it is already clear that if deletions become desirable, they should be made by codicil.

## INADVERTENT REVOCATION

A hazard to the uninformed is that a will may be revoked, in whole or in part, by operation of law. Triggering circumstances which radically (emphasize *radically*) alter the situation of testator include marriage, divorce, the birth of a child, sometimes the death of the principal beneficiary, or any other significant, unanticipated event.

Contracts not expressly mentioning a will may affect it. Chapter 8 discusses such contracts, beginning on page 224.

The risk of revocation by operation of law approaches nil if testator queries counsel when one of these unusual events occurs. Certainly it would be the burden of the attorney to recommend a new will if consulted about the key event or if, for example, an antenuptial agreement had been drawn or if counsel had participated in the divorce proceeding. But the lawyer cannot be blamed if testator has revealed nothing of the secret marriage or the divorce.

This rule of revocation implied by law is predicated upon the theory that because of changed circumstances, new moral duties rest upon testator, and it may be legally inferred that the will would have been changed had testator thought of it. In some states, this common law rule is preserved by statute. In others, it has been modified or even abrogated.

# THREE

# The Beneficiaries

When approaching the designing of a will, a testator faces many policy decisions. Fundamental to all of them are those pertaining to beneficiaries. These beneficiaries fall naturally into the following four groups: preferential, primary, secondary, and tertiary.

Almost always the basic purpose of a will is to make provision for people or charities. Used in a broad sense, the word "charities" includes churches, hospitals, schools, research programs, and all other recipients of testator's generosity, except persons and the very occasional corporate beneficiary, such as a fraternity, that is, the fraternity itself, which is not usually a charity, in contrast to its qualified

Educational Endowment Fund. After testator instructs in respect to beneficiaries, the rest of the will is really but a means to an end. It is devoted to establishing the legal machinery best suited to the attainment of the desired results.

## PREFERENTIAL BENEFICIARIES

In the eyes of the law, certain beneficiaries have such status that they must be willed a designated portion, or at least mentioned, to show that they have not been forgotten. They may be called preferential beneficiaries.

The legislatures require that a portion of the distributable estate as currently spelled out by statute pass to whom the law designates. In common law states, the wife's required portion was traditionally called "dower"; upon her husband's death she became a "dowager". The husband's reciprocal interest in his wife's estate was usually called "curtesy". Dower and curtesy amounted to from a third to a half the decedent's estate and sometimes varied with the nature of the property — real estate as against personalty. Both traditional rights are now largely superseded by what may be aptly called the "statutory share" of the surviving spouse.

A spouse who is willed less than the law requires may usually elect to take the statutory share despite the will. So, without a written agreement between husband and wife, a spouse should be left not less than the prescribed statutory share, no matter how much it irks testator to do so — unless it seems certain that for tax or other economic benefit, the survivor will not elect to take the statutory share.

Over a bridge table, a wife from a community property state might tell a dowager that she already *owns* half the family's property, hence has no need of a dower right to take effect upon death. If her husband has separate property and their community savings are not great, the community property wife should seek legal advice as to what her situation would be if her husband should fail to provide for her from his separate property.

Many states demand that certain other beneficiaries — usually children — be remembered but not necessarily left anything. Other states require that these primary beneficiaries be left to statutory proportion.

"I leave my three sons, Tom, Dick, and Harry, one dollar each and a like sum to each and every child who may be born to my wife Genevieve and me" is a clumsy way of showing you have not forgotten any child. I prefer the forthright:

Confident that their mother will well use our funds for their benefit, I make no direct bequest to our sons, Tom, Dick, and Harry, nor to any other child who may be born unto us. If my wife should predecease me, our children will receive under the trust herein established.

# PRIMARY BENEFICIARIES

Usually identity of the primary beneficiaries is self-evident: the members of the immediate family, sometimes including parents and siblings and sometimes not. Except in sad situations of estrangement, the dictates of duty and the desires of the heart coalesce. Yet, often the head must be called upon for rigorous consideration if divisions are to be wisely made.

## *Spouse*

A husband's first concern is usually for his wife, and vice versa. But what if the wife is independently wealthy, the estate of the husband modest, and his infirm mother without funds? Or the husband has a worthy child from a former marriage who will, it appears, always be near the poverty level. With the approval of the wife, might it not be right to put the mother or the child in the first line?

Or, again assume testator and his well-to-do wife have three children. Should the husband bequeath substantial properties to her, augmenting her estate (and taxes) and perhaps mingling his hard-earned savings with those of a future husband, a delightful fellow with five children and minimal financial resources? As a first reaction, an unqualified "No" would seem the proper answer. With her blessing, after token bequests to the wealthy wife, his estate should go directly to, or in trust for, the benefit of their three children.

On second thought, this is not so clear. "Wealth" is not often an absolute, as enduring as granite. Unless the wife's share of her family fortune is in solid, diversified assets irrevocably committed to her with abundant margins, present estimated value may prove ephemeral. So perhaps she should still be the first beneficiary of the trust, the children to receive the income as long as she has no need of it in order to live in her (husband's and wife's) accustomed fashion. On her death the corpus, the principal, of the estate will be distributed to their children or held for the education of their grandchildren as the testator directs. It is a basic rule that any formula which may result in rich or well-to-do children and an impoverished parent is to be eschewed.

Another and perhaps a better answer to testator's dilemma might be a "sprinkle" trust described in Chapter 5 (page 117), which is devoted to postmortem flexibility. The trustee would have authority to evaluate the needs of the surviving spouse and children and sprinkle the available funds where most needed.

### Children

Second only to the care of the surviving spouse come provisions for the education of the children. If the estate is modest in size, the natural formula is to leave it all to the surviving parent (or all in trust in the event of the death of both) and hope for the best.

Mention should be made here of the importance of instructions authorizing the trustee to invade principal to provide funds for educational purposes as well as to meet sickness or other emergency. Probably most parent testators will agree that until the children are, say, aged twenty-two (presumably through college), drafts on principal for the sake of one sick or injured child should be considered a family burden and charged against the estate as a whole, rather than against the recipient's proportionate interest in the principal of the trust estate. (After all, the children who were not sick or injured were the lucky ones!) Had both parents lived, an ambitious, bright child would be helped through college even though other children had no interest in things scholastic. But after adulthood, usually drafts on principal for a child should be a direct charge against that child's proportionate share of the principal.

Note that there has been no suggestion that a girl's share of trust *income* be curtailed merely because she marries before finishing school or a son's share of income be cut off because he prefers to go to work or to wander for a time.

Unless it is manifest that the decision should be otherwise, children should be treated equally. A child today off on a tangent may be the most responsible one a decade hence. As a parent approaches the final roll call, the aberrations of children may be seen in a more tolerant perspective. The impossible teen-ager or the arrogant know-it-all of the early twenties may evolve into a poised adult. Even though for a time the child was virtually disowned, if and when he or she settles down, usually this family member should be forgiven and should share in the family patrimony. The danger is that a punitive will unexpectedly may prove actually to be the *last* will. It has become too late to reinstate the disowned who now may well deserve to be included.

So, as to children, we start from the presumption that they should be treated equally. What is equality?

*Ruth, George, and Vincent:* Daughter Ruth married at the age of eighteen and her blue-collar husband has provided for her from that day on. Her father and mother financed her brother George during four years of college, three of graduate school, and two of postdoctorate training. True, he worked during vacations and, as time allowed, during the school year. All were proud of his erudition and the brilliant career in research believed to be before him. But viewed financially, George was a dependent nine years longer than was Ruth. His educational subsidy aggregated not less than $40,000.

The other son, Vincent, is an extrovert. He took two years of business training in a low-cost community college a few blocks from home. He volunteered for the Navy, returned with medals, and went to work as a salesman. He has prospered ever since.

If the family fortune is so great that $40,000 is not significant, it would seem appropriate for Ruth, George, and Vincent to share equally. But assume that the father's and mother's distributable assets, including life insurance, total no more than $150,000. Does share and share alike result in equal treatment? If Ruth and her husband, a mechanic, should face financial stringency, she might feel that George has been a favorite son —

receiving one-third of the estate plus $40,000, approaching double her share.

Vincent's two years at home after he had reached eighteen years of age should not be considered as a distortion. Ruth would have had the equivalent, perhaps more, if romance had not intervened. Perhaps their wills would seem right to the mother and father and, after discussion with the three children, to all of them, if they attempted equality with a provision stipulating:

It is our purpose as parents to treat our beloved children alike. Because of allocations made to George after he had completed his four years at college, I direct that my residuary estate be divided:

| | |
|---|---|
| To Ruth: | 40 percent |
| To Vincent: | 40 percent |
| To George: | 20 percent |

Result: George's present share would be about $30,000 plus the $40,000 educational subsidy, totaling $70,000. To Ruth and Vincent, each, $60,000. Or perhaps the percentages should be adjusted, bringing George down to a testamentary $20,000 and increasing each of the others' shares by another $5,000. Remember that George received $40,000 years ago when he needed it most and when money would buy more per dollar!

Let us shift George, Ruth, and Vincent to a different setting. Ruth marries into a family reputed to measure wealth in seven figures. Her husband has one sister, no brother. He is now a vice-president of the business established by his grandfather. People say that on his merits he deserves to succeed his father as president. Ruth has three children and a seemingly devoted husband. The bookworm George is less brilliant. He has civil service status in the reference room of a library; the probability is that he will be there until retirement. Again, Vincent is a productive salesman, but no one pictures him as sales manager.

This time the mother and father have about $180,000 to distribute among their three children. What is equity? What if librarian George has four or five children

— all adorable, much-loved grandchildren — and Vincent has none? Or what if the family business of Ruth's husband is highly speculative, believed to be worth no more than $100,000, and he has a playboy tendency?

With each variation, what would be fair provision for George, Vincent, and Ruth, and the education of the grandchildren?

What is equality? This time, think in terms of a disadvantaged child with a permanent physical or mental lack. He will always have to struggle to earn a bare subsistence. Is it equality to bequeath a modest estate share and share alike to him and well-situated siblings, or should special provision be made for him as long as he needs it?

Or consider, in still another family, the unmarried daughter Gertrude, age fifty-five, who has devoted most of her adult life to caring for an ailing, aging widowed mother? Should she not have preference over her two brothers, both with permanent, well-paying jobs? Here the following program might seem fair:

After directing disposition of usables and heirlooms, the mother's will establishes a trust. Income to Gertrude for life, with authority to trustee to draw on principal to care for her during sickness or emergency. On Gertrude's death, divide between the two sons, or to the children of a deceased son.

Under the principles to be stated in Chapter 6 (page 141), the two surviving brothers would not have been named the mother's trustees because of (1) conflict of interest with Gertrude, and (2) lack of training and experience in trust matters.

Illustrations of situations where mathematical equality does not bring justice between children might be multiplied indefinitely. The goal should be equity and fairness, rather than a precise dollar division. Still, except under truly special circumstances and forgetting old grievances, share and share alike is the natural formula for children. If possible, they should know and approve radical variations in advance. With a few well-chosen words, the will itself will tell why, thus taking care of the gossips.

Conscious that gifts may distort the distribution, some testators include a clause to this effect:

It is my intent to treat my four children alike financially, as nearly· as is feasible. To that end, if during any calendar year I should make gifts of money or other property (disregarding traditional gifts on Christmas and birthdays) to one child in excess of $500 over gifts made to my other child or children during that year, such excess over $500 shall be a charge against his or her interest in my estate.

If the estate is small, perhaps the limit should be $100. And if the estate is sizable, perhaps $1,000.

## Grandchildren

Coming to grandchildren, another problem presents itself. Bequests to them may be:

1. *Specific:* Here the grandchild is named and the will states what he or she shall receive. Grandmother's jewelry to the girls; grandfather's telescope and camping equipment to the boys. Specified amounts of money to all or some; if differences in money, a word of explanation why.

2. *Per stirpes:* "*Per stirpes*" refers to that mode of reckoning the shares of descendants whereby the children of any one descendant divide only the portion which their parent would have taken if living. As illustrated in the accompanying chart, son John's three children would receive John's share, one-third each. Son Richard's one child would receive all of Richard's share, three times the amount received by each cousin, the children of Uncle John. Daughter Ellen's six children would each receive one-sixth as much as Uncle Richard's son and one-half as much as each of their cousins born to Uncle John.

I have seen it distorted 11 to 1. You

guessed it. The grandchild with no brothers or sisters with whom to share had prosperous parents. The family with eleven children could barely pay the grocer.

While grandchildren are but potentials, not yet born, or if the variations in number among families are not radical, a *per stirpes* distribution usually seems the natural way. It is simply stated and sounds equitable — each through his or her own parents. Yet it is obvious that in some circumstances a *per stirpes* distribution may result in gross inequalities. "Why did granddaddy leave Cousin Jean nearly $20,000 and less than $2,500 to me?" The alternative is a *per capita* distribution.

3. *Per capita:* Bequests to grandchildren may also be *per capita.* The term defines itself; share and share alike. It is the antithesis of *per stirpes.* In the John, Richard, and daughter Ellen illustration just given, under a *per capita* distribution each of the ten grandchildren would receive 10 percent

of whatever portion of the grandparents' estate is earmarked for grandchildren. The chart on the following page illustrates.

The relative ages of the children may impose problems as the testator searches for the best way to treat his or her grandchildren alike. Suppose an age difference of fifteen years between the oldest and youngest child of testator; with a second marriage, it may be more. Suppose also that as testator studies the will plan, the youngest child is about thirty and the two older grandchildren are but little younger. At Halloween time, they are shepherding a new, a fourth, generation; no longer does testator think of these grandchildren as children; testator would like to have them receive their portions promptly after death comes — certainly when their own parents (testator's older children, now in their fifties) pass along.

Assuming great gaps in the ages of grandchildren in the second-generation families, for example, a grandfather-

# TEN GRANDCHILDREN
# PER STIRPES AND PER CAPITA
# DISTRIBUTIONS CONTRASTED

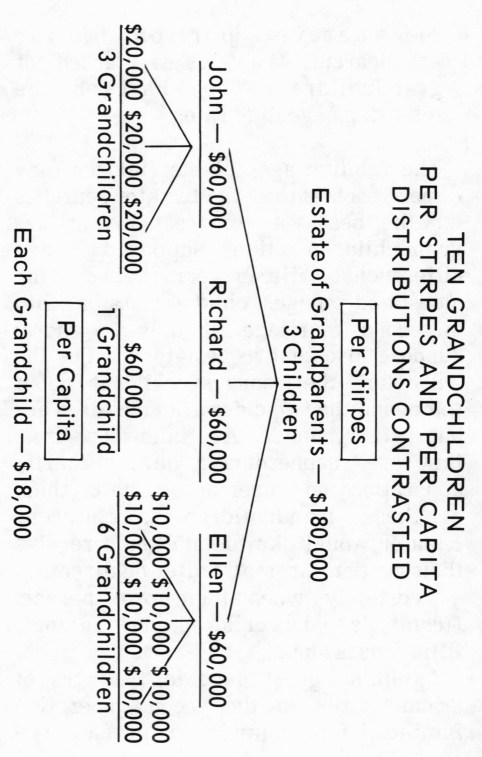

Estate of Grandparents — $180,000
3 Children

| Per Stirpes |
| --- |

John — $60,000

$20,000  $20,000  $20,000
3 Grandchildren

Richard — $60,000

$60,000
1 Grandchild

Ellen — $60,000

$10,000  $10,000  $10,000
$10,000  $10,000  $10,000
6 Grandchildren

| Per Capita |
| --- |

Each Grandchild — $18,000

64

testator, determined to treat his many grandchildren alike, might decide on something like this:

1. Upon his death a named amount to go to each of his children, or if a child should predecease him, then to the issue of that deceased child, *per stirpes*. The aggregate would be determined in relation to the size of the estate, but not so much that the basic *per capita* concept is thrown too much awry.

2. All the rest of testator's investment estate to be put in trust for the benefit of his children and their issue. As long as a child survives him, all the income shall be distributed to testator's children or to the issue of a deceased child *per stirpes*.

3. Upon the death of the longest-living of testator's children, the corpus to be divided share and share alike, *per capita,* among the then living grandchildren and, if there be a deceased grandchild leaving issue (great grandchildren), to such issue *per stirpes*.

Here there is a compromise: *per capita* as to corpus and *per stirpes as to income. To adjust income on a per capita* basis as to grandchildren would result in income inequality between testator's still-living children and could perhaps result in frequent changes, making the trust difficult to administer.

### Stepchildren

Families may be merged under many combinations of wealth and progeny. An affluent widower with three children marries a widow with two. With a brood of five, she must give up an excellent position. She has no capital. Or a wealthy widow with a child or two marries a charming college professor whose wife died, leaving him with four sons but no earthly possessions. Whatever the relationships of gold and children may be, as they establish a new family the parents want happiness for all. What financial arrangements should be made to take effect in the event of the death of either the bride or the groom?

This is particularly important where the children are quite young. Assuming confidence that the new marriage will work, it may be desirable for each parent to adopt the children of the other. Then the family is completely integrated, except perhaps as to property.

On a day-by-day basis, finances will not be a problem. But what in the event of the death of the rich spouse? At a surprisingly early age, the children may sense that one day some of them will be wealthy but the rest will have no more than a token inheritance. The situation could be complicated by a trust fund established by the deceased spouse of the rich stepfather or stepmother.

A vast financial imbalance between merging families invites consideration of a carefully drafted premarital agreement in respect to the testamentary treatment of all the children, including those who may yet be born. If some of the children are already well provided for under the will of their deceased parent, thought should be given to bequeathing a lesser fraction to these children of the wealthy parent, of course explaining why.

Often the specter of a possible divorce, however remote, lurks in the background. It may be extremely difficult to be wise — used here as a synonym of "fair." Future events may prove one wrong.

## SECONDARY BENEFICIARIES

The second group embraces brothers and sisters, cousins, aunts, and uncles — the clan — and occasionally, very special friends.

Here, I judge, there is no presumption of equality as there is among children. The actuality seems the opposite. Often, if not usually, there are good reasons why sharp distinctions should be drawn between secondary beneficiaries. When so doing, a word of explanation may seem justified. Testator, aged sixty-five, may say:

Because they are both well situated financially, I leave nothing to my sister Laura and my brother Herbert. I

68

bequeath the sum of $10,000 to my sister Margaret. Without imposing any limitation upon the use she makes of it, I express the hope that she will take a leave of absence from her work and enjoy a period of travel.

Or suppose Margaret is not the traveling kind. Her abilities are such that her big brother would not trust her with a substantial sum all at once. His will does not include a trust. He might instruct his executor to deposit $25,000 in a savings account, to be paid Margaret at the rate of $200 a month until the entire account, including interest, is consumed. If (as is likely) Margaret should die before the account is used up, the bank would pay the balance to a named charity or person.

In the majority of estates, even those bordering on the affluent, if there are several primary beneficiaries or their needs are great, only token bequests can be made to secondary and tertiary beneficiaries. In respect to them, the ultimate criterion is: Does testator feel that, under the circumstances of the estate, the will is fair?

In many instances, a "sprinkling" provision (Chapter 5, page 117) is a good way to provide for secondary beneficiaries as their needs arise.

## TERTIARY BENEFICIARIES

The third class of beneficiaries includes charities, projects, and people where there is no push of duty. Often the right amount is deemed to be a token bequest, not substantially affecting testator's fundamental plan. Only a minority of wills contain relatively large bequests to tertiary beneficiaries. The dollar test is: How much, without unduly diminishing allocations to primary and secondary beneficiaries, would testator like to give? The measure is subjective: the testator's pleasure at the thought of being able to help a hospital or to make a friend's later years easier.

Certainly not always, but often, a testator who plans to will significant sums for charitable, religious, or educational purposes is already so situated financially that he or she could have the pleasure of making the gift while still alive and save money by doing so. Suppose, for example, testator plans to devise his now seldom used $100,000 lakeside home and 5-acre recreational area to a church school. Instead of keeping his godly intent a semisecret until the will is read, he might reserve the guest house for his own use for life and deed an undivided one-fifth of the whole each year for five years as an *inter vivos* gift. The church could begin to use all (except that part reserved) at once. Income tax advantages would accrue. Each year there would be a deduction of $20,000 from donor's income because of this year's gift plus (if our illustration were an earning asset) somewhat less income on which to pay taxes because of the gift of previous years. If donor lives five years or more, the asset is entirely out of his estate; if he dies before the program is completed, the unconveyed portion would pass to the church under the will sans death dues.

A fairly complex type of gift was used as an illustration because of its possible suggestive value. The formula applies to securities and other assets. Instead of bequeathing 5,000 shares of General Motors to his school in his will, testator might give 1,000 shares a year and enjoy the tax benefits as well as the ovation he receives when the old boys gather.

As a testator considers gifts to charities, two practical considerations must season generosity.

First: If the eleemosynary bequest is more than nominal, there should be a percentage formula.

Unto Carmel Hospital I bequeath the lesser of the sum of $25,000 or five (5) percent of my net estate after payment of all claims, expenses, and taxes to which my estate is subject.

If, as testator expects, $25,000 amounts to no more than 5 percent, the hospital will receive the full $25,000. But if financial adversities preceded death and the net estate was reduced to $200,000, the hospital would receive $10,000.

Tax literature contains a classic

example. In the late 1920s, an immensely wealthy industrialist willed some $12,000,000 to various charities and the balance of his estate (he thought well over $150,000,000 after taxes) to members of his family and to trusts for their benefit. Came the 1929 crash and the economic disasters which followed. He died in 1931, leaving a net estate of about $10,000,000, all — and more — specifically bequeathed to named charities.

The second caveat (warning) is in respect to charitable remainders. Until recently, a natural pattern for charitable bequests was for a husband to leave his property in trust, with all the income to his wife during her lifetime and, upon her death, some or all the principal or income to named charities. Law books call this a "charitable remainder". Death dues were computed in relation to the life expectancy of the widow — that is, how long she would be using the income. The remainder would pass to the charities untaxed.

Overly astute people maneuvered the trust investments and income to reduce the amount the charity actually received. To plug this loophole, the Congress passed an act imposing strict requirements in respect to income distributions as well as to drafts on principal when there is a charitable remainder. Your attorney will use the precise technical language required by current regulations to carry your wishes into effect. (Charitable remainder trusts are considered in Chapter 12, page 375).

Here it would be unseemly to suggest the objects of your charitable bounty. However, it is proper to put down some fundamentals from the standpoint of the recipient. As far as is feasible within your, the donor's, objectives: *Impose no more restrictions than you feel you must.*

If the grant is for medical research, remember those who, a hundred years ago, limited their funds to smallpox and those who, a quarter-century ago, limited expenditures to polio. They were unduly restrictive.

If your bequest is to a school or church for capital expenditures, do not tell the trustees or deacons exactly what they must do with your money, unless you are pretty much financing the structure or wing. A memorial window would be an obvious exception. If your principal interest is aid to students, allow flexibility regarding scholarships and loans. Always be as broad in your instructions as your purposes will allow; you do not know what future needs will be. It is said that once there was a fund in St. Louis dedicated to providing new wheels for covered wagons en route west.

Sometimes the very organization to which a gift is made goes out of existence or radically changes its operations. In more than a hundred cities there are civic foundations — the Cleveland Foundation was the first — established to administer and disburse income and principal, as donors may direct, to worthy causes. This gives maximum flexibility to meet changing conditions. A generation ago a bequest to a foundation to be used for "boys work" would likely have been routed to a Boy Scout camp or improvements to a YMCA or Boys Club gym. Now, lacking indications from donor to the contrary, the trustees of the foundation might believe that funds within the broad designations of "boys work" could and should be channeled toward fighting drugs.

When testator has a loyalty to a church or school or other solid charity, the answer comes easily. There is no occasion to consider other channels. But when she or he does not, using a civic foundation as the disbursing medium (with one's favorite bank as trustee), testator's charitable funds can be kept abreast of changing needs.

Of course a family blessed with vast resources may create its own charitable trust or foundation. That is becoming a tortuous route, with tax and regulatory implications. These rare families will seek the guidance of experts.

## IDENTIFICATIONS; CHARITIES

It has been mentioned that testator should be unequivocally indentified. Similarly, there should be no vagueness as to beneficiaries. Usually the identity of "my wife" or "my son Jonathan" could not be mistaken. Nevertheless, the full name should be spelled out at least once so that "my wife" is introduced as "Carolyn Porter Thompson."

In some families, when it comes to nephews and nieces and cousins and friends, great care should be taken — there may be two or more of identical name, or of a name commonly used, like "Tom." Call him "Tom" if "Thomas" sounds stilted, but make it "Tom Griffiths, son of my brother Gordon."

Testator should be punctilious in identifying churches, charities, and causes when designating bequests. Names are often similar; brotherly love may not prevail if a substantial bequest hinges on an ambiguity. Recently, in Charlotte, North Carolina, the Grandfather Home for Children was the focus of litigation brought to determine whether certain existing institutions could take under a will which misnamed them. And who could be sure that a court would hold by "Boys Town of Nebraska" the benefactor meant "Father Flanagan's Boys Home"?

A will says: "I bequeath the sum of $10,000 to the Girl Scouts." Where should it go? To the local council? Or to the national organization? What means the term "The Congregational Church"?

## RESIDUARY CLAUSE

A tightly drawn will contains a residuary clause. It pertains to what remains after the rest of the estate has been used or distributed as directed in the will.

Akin is the paragraph which allocates properties if an expected line of succession should fail. Here, not infrequently, it seems natural to make a charity the beneficiary if testator's family should be wiped out. Let us consider an example.

Edith Lancaster, a widow aged seventy-three, faced the probability that her family line of succession would fail. Her perpetually ailing spinster daughter was fifty-two. Her happy-go-lucky, thrice-divorced son, aged fifty, had no children. The trim Mrs. Lancaster walked two miles a day and expected to live to the age of ninety, if not forever.

Her will provided for succession. The trustee bank was directed to distribute the income from her presumbly $300,000 estate equally between her two children as long as both should live. Drafts upon principal were strictly limited to meet dire emergencies.

If the son should die first, all the income would go to his sister. If she should go first, her share of the income would accumulate. Mrs. Lancaster remarked that she did not want her son to have more "drinking money." If he remarried and had a child or children of his own (not merely stepchildren or an adopted child), they were assured an education, but no more. This provision for unlikely grandchildren was given a temporary priority over the charitable remainder, next mentioned.

Upon the death of both her children without issue, or upon her death if she survived both as she fully expected to do, her entire estate would be held for the benefit of the Symphony Orchestra

Association to endow a chair, preferably that of first clarinetist, to be dedicated to Phillip, her son who had played that instrument in the high school orchestra. He had passed away many years earlier, at seventeen years of age.

# FOUR

# Exceptional Provisions

Nearly every combination of persons and property — the matériel with which wills deal — extrudes one or more problems which pose a challenge. What new plan can be formulated or how can a familiar provision be modified so that it will seem most likely to attain the desired goal?

Diversity in property and differences between people run such a gamut of variety that it would be impossible to draft a provision to meet every situation. Several testamentary directives, each designed to attain a specific result, have already been described, and in the chapters which follow this one, there will be many more.

Here are gathered a score of

suggestions, some of which may be adaptable to your problems. They have been loosely arranged into four groups: (1) personal; (2) pertaining to beneficiaries; (3) pertaining to property; and (4) family and public relationships.

## PERSONAL TO TESTATOR

### *The nurse or housekeeper*

In this family, the grandfather is almost helpless, particularly so since the grandmother died. No member of the family wishes to see him sent to a nursing home. Perhaps none is quite able (or willing) to take him in; and even though one were, he much prefers his own home and accustomed surroundings.

Housekeepers have come and gone, but Nora the nurse stood by the oldsters during the grandmother's long illness and indicates that, despite the monotony of the job, she might be willing to stand by as long as the old gentleman lives. What testamentary incentive can be given to hold her? A provision in the grandfather's will might state:

I bequeath the sum of $10,000 to my faithful nurse Nora Jones if she continues with me until my death.

This provision puts no premium on keeping him alive.

Before the will is decided upon, a written contract with Nora to this effect might be worth considering:

1. Monthly pay at the going rate for nurses.

2. A named semiannual bonus as long as she is competently caring for grandfather.

3. A provision in the will, executed and kept in effect, bequeathing Nora a specified sum for each year her patient lives.

Here we have a semiannual bonus; the incentive is not wholly dependent upon death; there is no clear invitation to arsenic. Yet, with each passing month the receipt of a substantial financial reward comes closer, and the reward itself is constantly increasing. After a time, Nora will have such an investment to preserve that there will be slight temptation to leave.

Expensive? Yes. But how much better, if the family can afford it, than taking the grandfather from his beloved home.

## Funeral arrangements

There is no requirement to this effect, but if a testator so decides, funeral and related mandates may be included in the will. However, frequently the will is not read until days after the grave is closed. So if testator's wishes are not a matter of family custom and knowledge, they should also be recorded elsewhere

There are many possible places to lodge specific instructions when the potential decedent has strong views on that subject. Because "he is out of town" has become such a frequent refrain, and because families and friends are often scattered, it is no longer eccentric for an oldster to record certain directions in duplicate or triplicate, leaving one here and another there. I know of a strong-minded dowager who travels so much that she cannot foresee where her end will come. She has arranged truly comprehensive coverage. Her sealed directives are in the hands of (1) her daughter, whose husband is in the foreign service; (2) her son, a colonel in the Marines; (3) the trust department of her bank; (4) a close friend; and (5) her lawyer. Incidentally, as is her prerogative, she seems to glean a certain gruesome glee from anticipating the shock which will hit her community of friends when her directions become known.

## Dissection of body

A few people, I believe increasing in number, wish to contribute to advances in the health sciences by making the body, or particular organs, available for the researchers in their laboratories. As in the case of funeral arrangements, a paragraph in the will alone may be read too late.

The nearby medical school or research hospital will probably have available printed forms designed to give the institution authority to use the body in its studies or to transplant an organ.

Next of kin should of course have advance information of testator's wishes in this regard. No opinion is here expressed as to what the courts of a particular state would rule if the surviving spouse or children abhorred the idea and refused to proceed, in defiance of insistence by the hospital or school. Some states, including New York, now have statutes which make possible the donation of one's body or particular organ.

## PERTAINING TO BENEFICIARIES

### Short life expectancy

There are varied circumstances under which a testator's inclination is to make a substantial lump-sum bequest to a relative or friend who has a short life expectancy. For example, a certain man's older sister Delores was as a mother to him; at age eighty-five, she has little beyond social security; "I would like to leave her $10,000, perhaps more. She does not travel; it is not a case of a gift for a trip around the world."

Testator has little use for his nephews, who neglect their mother. When they are called to his attention, he revolts at any risk of most of his $10,000 passing to them. If he is establishing a trust, the solution is simple. A first charge against the trust income would be a named sum each month to Delores as long as she lives or until she has received the specified maximum.

But what if testator has adult children and proposes to will all to them, share and share alike with no intervening trust? There are still several ways to provide for Delores:

1. *An Annuity:* Annuity contracts with no guaranteed number of payments are available. The beneficiary receives a certain number of dollars each month as long as she lives, and that ends it.

2. *A Bank Account:* As in the

illustration already given, the executor can be directed to establish a savings account in a bank with instructions to pay Delores a named sum each month as long as the deposit plus interest lasts, or while she lives. On her death, the balance, if any, is to be paid to a named charity or persons.

3. *In Trust to Sons:* The $10,000 can be willed in trust to his children with briefest trust powers, funds to be kept in a savings account, and payments to be made to Aunt Delores as stated in option 2, with balance, if any, distributed as testator prefers.

Under any plan, the will should direct that the program be put into effect as soon as legally feasible after the death of testator. Delores should not be required to wait one extra month.

Adaptations of these formulas may be preferable to lump-sum bequests for an invalid, or for the benefit of an unfortunate child with a short life expectancy, or for any other situation where it seems likely that the beneficiary will not long outlive the testator. Often, what the testator really has in mind is replacing (as it were, continuing) periodic *inter vivos* gifts he or she has been making.

## A handicapped or retarded child

The problems facing the parents of a retarded or handicapped child may be insuperable within the utmost periphery of the family resources. They can manage as long as both parents are active, the mother perhaps filling the role of nurse as well as wife and mother for the rest of the family.

But they are baffled as to the future. The funding of the income required for nursing care is beyond their means. And where can they find anyone to replace the parental love which the child so desperately needs? Reluctantly, an institution may be the only answer.

However, there are investigations regarding finance which the parents should make. The Department of Health, Education, and Welfare reports that nearly 250,000 persons receive social security benefits because they have severe disabilities which began in childhood and which keep them handicapped as adults. Depending on the circumstances, the child may be able to receive grants from one or more of a number of state and federal agencies:

1. The Department of Health, Education, and Welfare
2. The Old Age and Survivors Disability Insurance program under which a disabled child may be entitled to benefits
3. If either parent works for a railroad, the Railroad Retirement Act
4. A federal-state program of assistance known as Aid to the Permanently and Totally Disabled
5. Benefits under GI insurance policies and other veterans' benefit programs, such as Orphans Educational Assistance
6. Medicaid
7. Various state programs

The agencies, their names, and the relief available are in a constant flux. But not too far away will be an office of one of them which will survey the field with distressed parents and advise them as to strategy. These inquiries could result in provisions in the will which might not otherwise come to mind.

## The Spendthrift Clause

*Inter vivos* as well as testamentary trusts often include a paragraph ruthlessly entitled "Spendthrift Clause." I would rather designate it "Claims by Strangers." Your beneficiary may need protection against claims by third parties (a used-car dealer or peddler of penny oil stocks) without ever having been a spendthrift or sown more than the expectable number of wild oats. Proper provisions will insulate trust assets from claims by third-party creditors against beneficiaries of the trust, yet permit the trustee to provide for the necessary living expenses of the harassed beneficiary.

If you do include "Claims by Strangers"

protection, it should be expressly *in*applicable to those portions of the document establishing or relating to a marital trust. Otherwise, tax benefits may be lost. In Chapter 7 (page 198), more will be said regarding protective trusts.

### Expense of last illness and funeral of a legatee

There are times when a testator wishes to underwrite the expenses of the last illness and funeral of one or more beneficiaries. The underwriting may be limited to this particularized benefit, or it may be part of larger legacies. Wide discretion should be given the executor, the trustee, if any, or some person whose advice they are authorized to follow.

### Payments for beneficiaries under disability

During the life of the trust a beneficiary may be temporarily or permanently disabled. That beneficiary may, but likely will not, have a legal guardian to whom distributions may be made with the most orthodox formalities.

Testators often deem it wise to authorize the trustee, in his or her sole discretion (possibly after obtaining advice of a named individual), to make payments direct to those supplying goods or services to the beneficiary, or to a suitable person to pay certain of the ward's expenses. The trustee is entitled to protection against claims by the disgruntled if it should be asserted that the trustee was too generous. The trustee must of course act in good faith.

## PERTAINING TO PROPERTY

### A literary executor

Writers, composers, and artists should consider appointing a special literary executor with authority to handle matters affecting unpublished manuscripts, compositions, and artwork, as well as those already in stores or galleries. William Shakespeare neglected to do so;

his detractors assert that had he in truth authored the plays successfully staged during his lifetime and now attributed to him, he would have made some mention of them in his will.

The unworldly Ralph Waldo Emerson did much better. As his literary executor, he appointed his friend James Elliot Cabot, giving him meticulous instructions.

## Objets d'art

A family need not be wealthy to possess beloved *objets d'art* and heirlooms. To be classed with them for the purposes of this section are choice pieces of furniture, silver, and other items which should not be sold.

The period of possibly expensive storage may be shortened and the lives of the children enriched if the wills of the parents provide that in the event of the death of both of them, the trustee or guardian may make these things available for use by the children at an early age and will not be responsible for any loss or destruction by them.

## Her prized possessions

Many women have a multitude of things which should not be wholesaled into the residue of the estate. Sometimes madam wishes an item to go to a particular person. But it may be that she wishes to prevent its going to someone (perchance the next wife) by herself making a specific bequest.

Jewels and furs, of course, are *hers*. And usually most of the important usables in the house are legally as well as practically hers. The silver and best dishes were presents for the bride; the Steinway replaced the old Weber as her tenth anniversary present. The *objets d'art,* whether varied or a collection, were usually presents to the wife. Her own valuables should not be inventoried and taxed as part of her husband's estate.

The husband is likely to own almost no usables distinctly his own except bedraggled sports equipment. So, as she grows older, it is the wife who is inclined to make lists of specific bequests, perhaps too detailed.

Certainly the husband should have the use of all "her" furniture, furnishings, and household effects as long as he wants them. But the wife may well have wishes as to where items usable only by women should go upon her death and where her many other things should end after her husband discards them or is gone.

The four preceding paragraphs are orientation for the guidelines which follow:

1. *In the Wife's Will*

   *a.* The husband should be fully protected. All things which should be his absolutely or for life should be included in the will. When establishing a life estate, the passage can be delicately charted so that, on his death, her choice possessions go to *their* children rather than to his second wife and her children.

   *b.* Valuable single items or sets should be specifically described. "My three-carat diamond set with emeralds" should not be grouped with "my other jewelry." The antique Sèvres should not be a part of "dishes." This rule of description applies whether the bequest passes directly to the permanent beneficiary or pauses with the husband during his lifetime.

## 2. *In a Letter*

In many families a letter, changeable at home as one chooses, may dispose of all the cups and saucers and other things a woman loves to distribute in her imagination and perhaps redistribute among her changing favorites. The reference in the will should be about as follows:

Recognizing that it will not be of binding legal effect and that only this my will governs the disposition of my estate, I intend to leave a letter stating my wishes in respect to various items. I feel confident that all concerned will follow my wishes, even though not legally obliged to do so.

Then, my lady, rewrite the letter whenever the mood beckons, but be sure to destroy the previous instruction.

## Pets

One has a right to be a bit atypical. Adequate provision for loved pets is not an aberration to be disguised; it is a plan of which one may be proud. Care for pets must span three time zones: (1) immediately during the period of critical illness, the day of death, and therafter; (2) during the interim months of postmortem management; and (3) for the rest of the life of the pet. Sometimes one simple arrangement covers all. Sometimes not.

Obviously, as to (1), unless immediate care of the pet is implicit in the family or neighborly relationship, there should be an express understanding with someone.

In the will, the executor (or executrix) should be instructed as to what he (or she) should do. And the trustee should be told to carry on. As in the case of probably short-lived human beneficiaries, if a trust is established, there is no problem. The trustee can be directed to pay the bills, at least up to a specified ceiling. If there is no formal trust, perhaps the best way is a bequest to someone who also loves that particular pet or (second choice) that kind of pet with the understanding that it will be cared for.

The bequest paragraph may refer to the agreement regarding the pet. But since the pet cannot speak for itself and seek legal protection if its rights be violated, the plan is really an act of faith. The situation is rather like that of the letter indicating one's wishes in respect to usables. It is not part of the will itself, but probably will be followed.

### Personalty, specific bequests

Once you have determined to make a specific bequest, several attendant aspects should have your consideration. By "specific bequest" is here meant any bequest to a specified legatee of any item of personalty whether tangible or intangible (stocks, bonds, receivables, and rights of every description). Personalty includes everything but real estate (which will be considered shortly).

Assume that you have decided to bequeath to your cousin Laurene the 265 shares of the Second National Bank of Tareytown which you inherited from Aunt Grace. Do not be impatient when your attorney asks you: What if you sell the stock or the bank has been merged or dissolved before the time of your death, so that you own no stock in the Second National Bank of Tareytown; will you bequeath the equivalent in money? Where do stock dividends go, to Laurene or to your residuary estate? You say, "The 265 shares go to Laurene." What if Laurene predeceases you?

All these and other possible questions are but to suggest that there may be ramifications to specific bequests of intangibles. Or consider your car, a tangible.

I bequeath my Buick sedan to my sister Barbara and the Ford station wagon to Paul to use on his farm.

Bypassing the possibility of "which Paul," what does Barbara receive if the Buick has been turned in on a Mercedes-Benz? And what for Paul if the Ford was in a bad accident and was not replaced? When the bequeathed item is no longer in the estate, there has been an ademption. (See Glossary.)

### Real estate: specific devises

Questions ancillary to a specific devise (see Glossary) of realty may dominate the entire estate plan. Assume testator owns an apartment house, the value of which is about 40 percent of the entire estate. It is subject to a mortgage, say half its value. Rentals barely pay operating expenses and service the mortgage and taxes. Is the specific devise of the land and building to be subject to the mortgage — what if the death occurs when business is bad and there are many vacancies? Or is it testator's intent that the devisee receive the property free and clear? If so, the mortgage debt will be a liability of the residuary estate.

Whenever there is to be a significant specific grant (real or personalty), think it through, both as to the effect upon the recipient and from the standpoint of the estate as a whole. All who are to receive under the will will be affected.

Special care may be necessary if the supposed real estate is no more than a contract under which you, the testator, are buying a property and the contract does not carry itself. Or if you are buying the Buick at so much a month with $2,000 still owing.

## Use of home

Not infrequently a testator must decide: How shall I devise our home or my interest in it? To my wife (or husband) direct, outside the trust? Or to my testamentary trust?

If the decision is to route the home through the trust, testator should be specific regarding the burden upon the trust and the beneficiary in respect to: (1) payment of taxes; (2) major repairs; (3)

routine maintenance, including garden if that is a significant expense; (4) insurance coverage; and (5) waiver or payment of rent.

Testator should also consider the wisdom of provisions for sale of the home if the survivor should wish a different setting. Perhaps the trustee should be authorized to buy a house or condominium which the survivor deems more suitable than the old place echoing with memories.

## *Forgiveness of debt*

Occasionally a testator wishes to forgive a debt. If the intent to forgive is not blazoned on the will, it becomes the duty of the executor to collect the last farthing and to pay taxes on this asset of the estate. It might have been wise planning to forgive and forget — to cancel the note, if any — before death. If the amount involved is of consequence, the routines of making a gift by forgiving the indebtedness should be reviewed with counsel and testator's accountant.

# FAMILY AND PUBLIC RELATIONSHIPS

## *Family Ownerships*

These paragraphs are a recognition of the fact that the ancient rule of primogeniture was not entirely without merit. That was the preference in inheritance which was given by law or custom to the eldest son and his issue or, rarely, to the line of the eldest daughter. The principle maintained the family status through succeeding generations.

There is a modern application. Assume a family business built up by the grandfather and carried on by his two sons — "York and Sons, since 1906." The grandfather's daughters were provided for with outside funds; he wanted no in-laws intruding in the family business. The progeny of the two sons are six in number. Two, a man and a woman, are now the key executives of York and Sons. The other four are on their own.

The two brothers, now very senior second-generation, might well give consideration to a joint program which would keep ownership or at least voting control of York and Sons in the two third-generation managers. Counsel and the accountant will be able to suggest paths suitable to the occasion.

## Public policy

Some testators succumb to the temptation to make the will an occasion for denouncing the members of the family. In most instances — I would guess — despite their attorney's advice to the contrary.

One so tempted should remember that, though signed perhaps a decade before death, the will may well be testator's last public statement for the world to read and his or her last discussion with members of the family. It may be considered a measure of its author rather than of those whom testator indicts. And a wrong which may have been real ten years before the will is read may no longer have verity and its atonement may be long since complete.

A will is no place for vindictiveness or

the recording of punitive action. This is not to say that testator should route funds to persons or institutions who, the maker believes, should not receive them. So we come to another delicate point.

## Disinheritances and notable discrepancies

It has already been seen that a spouse and, in a few jurisdictions, children receive a statutory minimum even though testator wishes otherwise. Usually, or at least often, there are other heirs who would also share were there *no* will. The testator who has a right to bequeath also has the corollary right not to bequeath — to disinherit. Except for children and others prescribed by statutes, there is no legal requirement to call attention to the fact that nothing is bequeathed to nephew Ned. The will is silent as to him, that does it.

But what if there were a parcel of nephews and nieces to whom an indulgent uncle left $5,000 each — except to Ned. Was it an oversight? Any uncle can forget one out of eight when suddenly asked to name the children of his brothers and sisters. Or was the omission of Ned's name purposeful? If so, why? Tongues chatter. Ned's young lawyer-friend sees the potentials of a will contest.

As a legal caution, Ned should have been mentioned, but graciously. If a disinheritance should be a matter of record, it should be so worded that credit attaches to testator and no harm is done the disinherited — except to miss a bequest. Usually there will be a valid, explainable reason. Perhaps Ned is already wealthy. If he is unable to think of a pleasant reason, testator can show that he did not forget Ned by saying: "After careful thought, I have determined that it is better not to include a bequest to my nephew Ned."

The remarks regarding disinheritances apply also to notable discrepancies between several beneficiaries of the same class — brothers and sisters, for example. The testator may wish to draw sharp distinctions based on several factors — financial position, children to educate, health, age, and so on. The fact that one is a favorite need not be mentioned; nor that the youngest brother to whom but a token was left is a rounder and a disgrace to the family. The lawyer is being well paid as a ghostwriter for the testator to put down the words of a gentleman.

## No-contest provisions

Not infrequently a testator inserts a clause or two providing that if anyone contests the will, he or she shall receive some trivial named amount or be cut off entirely. If the atmosphere is such that fear of a contest is more than neurotic, the no-contest clause should be most carefully drafted in light of the laws of the applicable state or states. They differ; some are quite strict as to the prerequisites to an enforceable provision. For example, some states require a "gift over," that is to say, the legacy forfeited by the contestor, must go to a named person or class of persons, such as "my brothers and sisters." That the assets in limbo would go to the residuary estate may not be enough.

Do not nonchalantly include language such as:

If any heir or any other person or any institution should contest this my will or any part thereof, I bequeath each contestant the sum of ten (10) dollars.

This does not guarantee that you have tightly locked the barn door.

If you believe your situation does include elements of danger: (1) Ask your lawyer how the no-contest provision should be molded to your family needs under the laws of your state. (2) Consistent with what has gone before, be tactful in the way you say what you believe should be said in your will. Kind words just might divert the irritated potential contestant.

### *Excessive eccentricity*

When discussing pets, I urged the prerogative of being atypical. Subject of course to the fetters of public policy, every testator may and should express duly determined wishes. But good judgment should be used. The heading of this short section is *excessive* eccentricity. Moderate eccentricity is, I think, delightful. When drawing wills, there are at least two arguments against excessiveness.

The less important is that it may make testator look a fool when no longer here to correct (or confirm) that dour impression.

The more important is that should there be a will contest, excessiveness may influence the judge or jury to decide that the testator was not competent. So, much as you might enjoy doing so, do not go too far off center when drawing a document you will not be present to support.

The ultimate in eccentricity is a testator who vents spleen by libeling someone. Appellate courts have held that offering the will for probate is a publication (that is, third parties learn of it), which makes the estate liable to the person or persons defamed. Illustration:

I leave nothing to my grandson because he squandered a large gift, deserted his mother, and was a slacker in World War II.

The Supreme Court of Oregon held the estate liable for the defamation. Otherwise, it said, persons defamed in a will would be helpless in violation of the Oregon constitution which affords every one a remedy for an injury done to one's reputation. Some other jurisdictions would exonerate the estate.

When presenting the will for probate, the executor acts as an officer of the court and is seldom held to account for the contests of the will.

## FIVE

# Postmortem Flexibility

As is implicit in several of the illustrative powers already or later noted, considerable discretion may be, and often should be, granted to the trustee. Power to use principal to finance an emergency or a child's education and to divert income from comfortably situated siblings to care for a handicapped brother or sister is common. Here we will consider four ways to authorize the making of depositive determinations (who receives the money and under what circumstances) *after* testator is gone. The four methods are (1) by power of appointment; (2) by "sprinkling"; (3) by accumulation trust; and (4) by a flexible education program.

We now look at authorizations by the testator which enable others to make fundamental decisions one might think of as reserved to testator alone. Testator empowers others, as it were, to write or rewrite critical segments of the will as they deem wise. A man, for example, is in effect saying, "I prefer to have the decision as to the division between our children made by my wife when the children are mature; I see only adolescents."

## A POWER OF APPOINTMENT

A power of appointment is an authority conferred by will or other proper instrument upon a person (the "donee" or "holder" of the power) to determine who is to receive property or the usufruct — the income — thereof after the termination of named interests. Carefully read a second time, this terse definition will be seen to describe a legal device which may be very useful. For example:

The testators, in their late fifties, have one son, two daughters, and several grandchildren. The husband is not well and the prognosis is discouraging. He and his wife are well situated financially but are not rich. There will be plenty to provide for the wife, presumably without draining principal. What should the division be after her death? She may outlive her husband by twenty-five years.

At the moment, their son Harold, aged thirty-one, is not drinking. After his divorce six years ago, he drifted and for a time confirmed most of the evil things his former wife had tearfully recounted. She had custory of their only child and her second, very satisfactory husband would gladly adopt the little girl, but Harold will not give his consent. He insists on the weekly visit as provided in the decree of divorce. As of today, the testators simply do not know to whom their combined estates should go after both of them have passed away.

How much to their formerly wayward son whose pattern of life they cannot confidently predict? How much to their older daughter with four children, her husband a blue-collar worker in a cyclical industry? What proportion to their younger daughter who married the architect and has no children?

A partial solution is a limited power of appointment in each will. A limited power prescribes the persons or classes of persons who are to receive the property. In contrast, a general power places no limitation upon the donee when appointing the ultimate recipient of the fund.

The husband's trust could provide for the wife for life and give her authority to appoint any of their three children and their issue in respect to the disposition of his estate upon her death. Her will would be the converse. The two powers may be of great psychological value to the testators as they seek to guide and aid children and grandchildren. It may be a good thing for black-sheep Harold to know that, though his father is gone, his mother can still cut him off in toto if he does not keep his ways mended.

Hence, if the gloomy forecast of the doctor should prove justified and the husband should soon depart, the final decision as to how his estate is to be divided among his children, grandchildren, and perhaps great-grandchildren would be deferred as long as the wife lives and is competent to make a will — a long time, according to the life expectancy tables.

A moment back, the power of appointment was referred to as a partial solution to the problems facing these two testators. It would prove of no efficacy if both should be lost in a plane crash. Their current wills must also reflect their best present decision.

The holder of a power of appointment owns a valuable right. The disposition of property is put within donee's control. Someone may say, "I will pay you $10,000 cash tomorrow if you will appoint me as your successor as beneficiary under Uncle Harry's trust." If a general power (that is, the power to appoint whomever the holder wishes), the power is taxable in the estate of the holder. If a power is sufficiently limited (as "among my descendants"), not so.

The definition at the beginning of this section refers to the power as "conferred by will or other proper instrument." A living trust would be an appropriate instrument within which to include a power of appointment.

## Sprinkling

"Sprinkling" is a colloquialism referring to a power given to a trustee to use its discretion when allocating and distributing income among two or more beneficiaries. A New York court spoke of the trustee's authority "freely to sprinkle the income" as if the trustee "were playing a hose" among the members of trustor's family. A typical provision limited to children might read:

In its sole discretion, trustee may use or distribute so much of the income up to the whole thereof as the trustee deems advisable for the maintenance, health, and education of my children. Distributions for or among the beneficiaries shall be without limitation as to equality. Income not so distributed shall be added to the principal.

117

Sprinkling has a triple purpose:

1. It gives postmortem flexibility; trust income will be more apt to reach those beneficiaries who need it most.

2. It is an additional barrier against the creditors of beneficiaries. (See "The Spendthrift Clause," Chapter 4, page 91, and "Protective Trusts," Chapter 7, page 000.)

3. It is a useful tool in reducing the aggregate family income tax. Illustrating this aspect: Assume a large estate; the father's trust will yield $30,000 a year, upon which the recipients must pay taxes measured by income. The mother has separate property; she reaches a high tax bracket.

If the trustee were given authority to spray the income as deemed best, son Harrison, while in medical school, could be financed direct from the trust without the funds flowing through the mother's accounts and adding to her taxes. The same may be said of subsidies to all the children.

The typical provision, given near the beginning of this discussion of sprinkling, demarks testator's children as the class within which sprinkling is authorized. It need not be so tightly limited. The surviving spouse and others may be included. However wise it may be to include mother or father along with the children, a natural reaction on the part of the parent-testators is an emphatic "No" — even in a situation where there is a potential for a considerable saving in taxes. What matron, for example, wants some young trust officer deciding how much she shall receive?

When the trust estate is modest in amount, sprinkling among parents and children may lead to conflict between generations. Not so if both parents are gone. The more limited the resources of the estate, the more important it may be for the trustee to have utmost latitude when sprinkling in order to do the best possible job in financing the orphaned children.

Sprinkling may also be an excellent method for the channeling of the funds of the testators to grandchildren and great-grandchildren whose needs cannot yet be envisaged, including babies who may be born after the death of testator. Bachelor Uncle Robert may see sprinkling as a way to spread his largess among the family.

The sprinkling authorization may be restricted by guidelines. It may be "not to exceed" a named sum per annum per beneficiary, or it may be limited to the "children who are in school or college." In your will, be clear; does "college" include medical school?

## ACCUMULATION TRUSTS

The trustee may be instructed to withhold income within the trust instead of disbursing it to beneficiaries. Income accumulates in the trust subject to instructions; this maneuver results in what is commonly referred to as an "accumulation trust." A principal purpose may be to save on income taxes, an objective that will again be mentioned in Chapter 12 (page 340). Here we look at it as a device which permits an additional postmortem flexibility.

Testator instructs that trust income, or a named or optional proportion thereof, be retained in the trust. The instruction might earmark it generally as an educational fund for great-grandchildren; or as an emergency fund to use in case of accident or illness. Or there may be no directive as to time and purpose of drafts upon the accumulated reserve, leaving the decision to the wisdom of the trustee. Or the instructions regarding disbursement of accumulations may be so tightly drawn that little or no new discretion is exercised.

In contrast, a will might reach the ultimate in postmortem flexibility by a judicious combination of (1) power of appointment to route principal to its ultimate recipients, (2) sprinkling to vary the distributions of income, and (3) an accumulation authorization permitting or directing the building of reserves for whatever purpose testator designates.

# A FLEXIBLE EDUCATIONAL PROGRAM

Assume a situation similar or analogous to this: A wealthy widowed woman has two daughters and nine grandchildren, aged four to fifteen. Daughter Marie, the mother of five, is divorced. She receives sporadic support money. Daughter Lillian, mother of four, once a widow, is happily remarried to a prosperous doctor. If her husband lives and continues to thrive, the education of her children will not be a financial problem. But if the doctor should be incapacitated or if, as before, Lillian should lose her husband by death, desired schooling might be in jeopardy.

As things stood as of the day the will was signed, Marie's five children would need substantial subsidy if a complete education were to be made available to each of them. But, like her sister, Marie may yet enjoy the blessing of a financially secure second marriage. As testatrix points out, the cycle may turn and Lillian's brood be the one in need of educational funds.

How can flexibility be obtained, operative after the grandmother is no longer here to open her purse when she thinks best? One answer is to spell out a possible article for her will. Her instructions will be repeated not only to show a possible handling of perhaps the most frequent of all crystal-ball problems (the education of unpredictable children) but also to illustrate how the sprinkling principle can be adapted to testator's wishes for the watering of any garden. This woman's directive reads:

I hereby establish an Educational Trust of $250,000 separate and apart from my residuary trust. The purpose of this Educational Trust is to provide a backlog fund to assure the education of all my grandchildren. By education, I mean more than mere presence at school, whether it be high school or college. I mean devotion to an educational project which should lead to a constructive career.

Allocations from my Educational

Trust to a grandchild who is in school are not to be on a per capita basis. They are to be made in relation to the needs and potentials of the child. My policy has always been and still is to treat my daughters and their children as nearly alike financially as is feasible. Nevertheless, if there were a capable grandchild anxious for a professional education I would not hesitate to assist that child as a family enterprise without counterbalancing gifts to the others. My two daughters have both experienced vicissitudes and I cannot foresee what the future will bring to either group of grandchildren. So I am here treating them as nine children going through the educational process, all my grandchildren and each entitled to consideration from me.

The decision as to distributions shall be that of the trustee. When, in its discretion, it makes a decision as to disbursements, it will not be subject to challenge by any beneficiary or other person. The trustee and whatever advisers it chooses to consult shall consider the scholastic record of the child, his apparent adaptability to whatever education he has in mind, his zeal and record for diligence, his *personal conduct* and all other factors which, in the judgment of the trustee, have a bearing upon whether or not this grandchild should receive a special subsidy.

If funds remain in the Educational Trust after all of my grandchildren have completed their educations or reached the age of twenty-five years (whichever event first occurs), such funds shall be poured into the residuary trust, share and share alike, for each family, as therein provided. A special reserve may be established for a beneficiary in military service.

The testatrix's educational trust may be classified as a sprinkling trust with instructions. The guidelines she established illustrate the instructions which may be given any sprinkler in respect to providing funds to meet all manner of problems and projects —

straightening teeth (up to $3,500 extra for any child); the building or buying of a home; worldwide travel for the budding architect; prolonged illnesses when more than one beneficiary may need, or be asking for, a greater subsidy; any imaginable tribulation or opportunity.

# SIX

# Selecting Fiduciaries

The substantive provisions of the will are your directives in respect to the management and disposition of your property and the care of beneficiaries. But your mandates are not self-executing. Someone must put them into effect. The wisest of instructions may fail if not stated in the framework of suitable legal machinery, the operation of which is entrusted to proper hands. So when, in this chapter and elsewhere, I discuss the mechanics of handling an estate, I am not departing from the basic theme — the making of wise provisions in respect to your properties and your loved ones.

As lawyers use the word, a "fiduciary" is a person or institution acting for, or

127

taking the place of, another. (See Glossary.) Fiduciaries substitute. This chapter will discuss the choice of fiduciaries whom testator may nominate to serve as representatives after death requires it. These include (1) an executor or executors; (2) a guardian or guardians of the person of minors or incompetents; (3) a trustee or trustees. And in addition, (4) testator's lawyer. Consideration will also be given to removal of trustees.

## ON CHOOSING THE EXECUTOR

An executor, it will be recalled, is a person or institution appointed by any testator in the will to carry out the terms of that will. A woman would be an executrix. Either one serves until the estate has been distributed to the beneficiaries or trustee, or in part to both. The executor's duties are summarized in Chapter 9.

Until advancing years of illness take their toll, the husband is the natural personal representative (executor) of the wife's estate and she of his. Not infrequently, a wife untutored in business affairs prefers not to serve. Or perhaps she will confidently serve only as coexecutrix with their adult son or daughter or with her husband's brother or with hers — if the husband is inclined to appoint him. Or with a bank as coexecutor. Possible variations are many. Preferably with the consent of all adult beneficiaries and subject to the approval of counsel for the estate, a novice executor or executrix may employ a bank to perform many of the chores of administration.

Neither skill nor stability should be sacrificed to save fees, but the fact remains that if either husband or wife is competent to do the tasks ahead, the cost of postmortem management may be greatly reduced. This is partly because the question of whether a surviving husband or wife should accept compensation for managing the estate is a matter of arithmetic — relative taxes.

If the wife violates the American tradition and goes first, the husband can continue his accustomed income-earning activities. No longer able to file joint income tax returns, his income taxes skyrocket. If he is paid for his services as executor, he will receive new income taxable at his highest rate. Unless the wife's estate is very large, the reduction in death dues by reason of fees paid to the executor will be more than offset by the increase in his own taxes measured by income. A waiver of all fees by the executor-husband is often indicated.

In contrast, consider the situation when the wife is executrix. The husband's earned income has ended. Assume she has no personal income. Here, perhaps, she should accept a fee as large as the court will allow, stretched out over two or three years, thus reducing the taxes of the estate without pushing her into a high income tax bracket.

If a competent individual or combination of individuals is not available, a bank stands ready. The trust departments employ personnel trained to perform the services required of an executor. Most trust officers have a kindly approach to the problems of their beneficiaries. Sometimes they are called "social service workers for the affluent." Later, when discussing the choice of trustees, I will say more about the advantages and disadvantages of perdurable corporate fiduciaries as compared with transitory individuals.

Using the wife's will as the illustration, a natural succession of executors might be:

## Pattern A
### (First will)

I appoint my husband John as my executor. In the event of his death, inability to serve, or preference not to serve, then the Bank shall succeed him.

## Pattern B
### (Beginning at about age 60)

I appoint my husband John and our son Richard as coexecutors. In the event of the death, etc., of either of them, the other shall serve alone. In the event of the death, etc., of both of them, the Bank shall serve as sole executor.

## Pattern C
### (Perhaps an alternative)

I appoint my husband John and our son Richard as coexecutors. In the event of the death, etc., of either of them, the Bank shall be joined as coexecutor, it to serve alone in lieu of both of my individual executors if occasion should demand.

## Pattern D
### (At age 80)

With his full concurrence, desiring to relieve my husband of burdens incident to the probate of my estate, I appoint our son Richard (with succession as in Pattern A, or appoint Richard and the Bank, the latter to serve alone if necessary).

And of course, as already indicated, brothers, sisters, partners, friends, or others may be designated to serve in appropriate sequence to the end that testator's affairs be kept in the hands of persons of his or her choice as long as is possible. Or testator may prefer to name the bank as first and sole executor. The ultimate question for testator to answer is: "Who can best handle my affairs between my death and the distribution of my estate in accordance with my will?" If there is a going business, consideration should be given to naming a business associate as a coexecutor. Or to instructing the executor to seek the associate's advice. But as will be stressed when discussing choice of trustees, such a person may have an adverse interest.

Choosing the executor is rather like deciding upon a short-term, emergency manager for a business, whether large or minute. In contrast, when selecting the trustee, a very long-term aspect may enter.

You will notice that an executor, a trustee, and the guardian of property may be a person, or persons, or a corporate institution (a bank or trust company), or a combination of them. Hence, as the context happens to go, the pronoun reference has been and will be "he," "him," "she," "her," "they," "them," or frequently "it."

## ON CHOOSING A GUARDIAN

There are two kinds of guardian: guardians of property and guardians of the person. Here we speak of the latter. If your will creates a proper trust, it is unlikely that a guardian of property (often called a "conservator") will be required, although occasionally there can be substantial savings in income taxes by the establishment of another taxing entity. But you should not overlook the too-often forgotten provision nominating a guardian of the *persons* of your children in the event of the death of both you and your mate. Occasionally it may be seemly to nominate a guardian of a senile or incompetent parent or other person who is to benefit from the will.

You do not usually have power to designate a guardian of the person in the sense that you appoint a trustee or an executor. You nominate a guardian; the court appoints him or her. But the wishes of parents or of sensible people closest to the child will usually be followed, unless the judge deems it manifest that the best interests of the ward (the child) will be served by disregarding the recommendations.

Assuming the death of both parents, it is not unusual to select a guardian outside the family. It may be no reflection on relatives to do so. Consider three small children, aged three to seven. Their maternal uncle (mother's one brother) is a bachelor. The father has two sisters and a brother. One sister has already had a divorce and her second marriage is turbulent; her children have had an unhappy time and would not be good cousins with whom to grow up.

The father's (the testator's) other sister is an unmarried, very intense professional worker. His brother is a successful businessman with four children and a socially minded wife. Three grandparents are living. All are devoted to the children, and the children to them. But the age gap is too great.

Where, within the family, can a suitable

guardian of the *persons* of the children be found? Almost any bank with a good trust department can manage the property. Mothering and fathering the orphaned children, nursing them through the measles, and guiding them during the difficult teen-age years is a more sensitive assignment. Indeed, usually a bank is not eligible to be guardian of the *person.*

It is most important that in a situation such as here described, the parents choose — if you please, from time to time rechoose — the collateral relatives or the friends most likely to be the best available foster parents. Otherwise, the least suitable of all distant relatives may suddenly develop a deep sense of affection (heretofore not visible) and a conviction of a duty to rear the bereaved children — especially if no financial problem exists and their presence would in fact subsidize the household. Of all the decisions a testator makes that of the children's guardian may be the most important.

The first reaction is to ask whether your nominee would be willing to serve as guardian. That should not be done without first considering possible results: (1) Do you want someone to serve as guardian merely because a decade prior to your deaths, that friend agreed to do so? Should not the test be whether your nominee is ready, able, and willing to serve when the sad day arrives to take over — not as of the moment of a chat long before, perhaps almost forgotten? (2) Conditions change; new friends are made; previously steady people go on tangents. Will you feel as free to nominate other guardians if you have, as it were, a commitment from those already asked?

Believing that, for young children, the most natural and most desirable guardians are usually found in a similarly situated friendly family with children of about the same age as testator's, I suggest the desirability of nominating alternative families, varying your nominees as conditions change. If you have not asked permission to nominate, you will not have to apologize and try to explain why you have withdrawn the designation. Or, worse still, you will not drift along with a worrisome nominee named in your will because of the embarrassment incident to repudiating those first chosen.

I said "named in your will." Unless the nominee is the obvious first choice and the alternate (if any) an obvious second choice, I do not favor any nomination *in the will itself*. I prefer to put it in a codicil first executed immediately after the will has been signed and changed from time to time as conditions change. Here it must be remembered that the death of both parents is far less likely than the death of one. If either papa or mama survives, there will be no occasion for a guardian of the persons of the children. There will be no need to tell the world whom you had in mind to act in the remote event both parents should be lost. If you have nominated maternal Aunt Helen and her husband, the children's paternal Uncle Theodore and his wife Emmy may (1) be honestly and openly relieved, and offer to help; or (2) be secretly relieved, but put on a show of hurt that the in-laws were chosen.

If the codicil directs that it is not to be presented for probate except in the event of the death of both parents, no one need know who was designated until two deaths make it necessary for all to know. Thus, the surviving spouse retains the option to nominate updated guardians without the first choices ever becoming a matter of family discussion. Only your lawyer, whose lips are professionally sealed, will know.

In contrast to this unorthodox suggestion of not informing prospective guardians of the person, usually the opposite would be true as to executors and trustees.

Within your financial limits, the codicil should clearly instruct the trustee that your children are to be no financial burden upon their guardians. Your estate permitting, the trustee should be generous in this regard. It should be authorized to provide adequate help for the new mother, suddenly inundated with your children; for example, to provide money to build an additional bedroom and bath, it being recognized that the addition will become a part of guardian's realty. I know of a trustee bank which wisely furnished the guardians of five children with funds sufficient to build a wing to the guardians' home — five bedrooms plus two baths for the three boys and two girls. That investment paid fabulous dividends as and after the children adjusted to the trauma of losing both parents. (Incidentally, those guardians were strangers to the blood.)

Certain young testator parents who enjoyed inherited wealth had three small children. They felt that by far the best present choice for guardians would be the nearby parents of playmates of testators' youngsters. The favored family was on its own financially; the mother worked. Testators thought it wise to include in their codicils:

There is no way in which I can adequately compensate the personal guardians of my children. Nevertheless, if the guardians' circumstances should be such that it would be of benefit to them to accept compensation, the trustee is authorized and directed to pay them or either of them a reasonable sum for services in addition to the out-of-pocket costs incident to the care of my children.

This would enable the young mother who suddenly has five children instead of two to give up her downtown job without sacrifice to her own family. If the size of testator's estate is great, the word "generous" might well be substituted for "reasonable."

## ON CHOOSING TRUSTEES

In the first chapter, it was recognized that frequent references would be made to "trusts" and "trustees." The reader unfamiliar with these terms was invited to divert and read Chapter 7, which tells about trusts as trusts. That is now the very next chapter. If you feel you would like more background regarding trusts generally before considering the vital question of choice of trustees and their line of succession, Chapter 7 is handy. But if you jump forward, do not fail to return. You do not want to entrust your financial affairs to the wrong manager.

Much of the discussion pertaining to the selection of an executor applies to the selection of a trustee, having always in mind significant differences in functions. The span of time the *executor* serves will range from a year, or perhaps less, to usually not more than two or three years unless, for tax or other advantages, it is deliberately decided to keep the estate open longer. In sharp contrast, the *trustee* may serve a long time; indefinitely, if a charitable trust is established. To solve the duration problem, if the testator so desires, an individual may be the first trustee or cotrustee, with a bank as a certain or contingent successor.

An important consideration in respect to choice of executor or trustee is the probability of the availability of your nominee. In relation to human life and business risk, a sound bank is immortal. It will not move away. If it merges, its trust functions will continue. Even if it should fail, its trust department will be held segregated from its commercial activities and the trust operation will carry on. An important decision is not the whim of a single trust officer; it is the composite opinion of a trust committee. No individual can offer similar assurance of stability.

Fortunate testators may choose members of the family to be trustees of the family properties, or of some of them, with succession as already illustrated for executors. Assume the will of the husband whose estate will be in the order of $150,000. His wife is his first concern. He does not desire to continue a trust beyond her death. They are blessed with two staunch children, both seemingly permanently located within a day's travel of the family home. Despite his confidence in them, the father does not want to give the children complete control over their mother's financial affairs. Nor does he want to scar their relationships with disagreements over the management of property or over the propriety of drafts on principal for their mother's account.

He cannot ignore the possibility that his son and daughter might be too much influenced by covetous spouses.

He might feel safe if he named his wife and children as cotrustees (of course with the bank as a backup), with tailored instructions covering (1) voting, and (2) bringing in the bank as a neutral trustee.

*Voting:* Testator might instruct that a vote by the wife plus that of either child will control, but the vote of the two children cannot overrule that of their mother. Mother has negative power on her vote alone.

*A Neutral Trustee:* Without mother and children recognizing any fault, communications may break down. Indeed, as she grows older, it may become impossible to talk business with the mother. Perhaps she cannot understand why she is not free to travel as much or as elegantly as do some of her widowed friends. So testator provides that at any time, at the request of the mother or of the children or either of them, the bank shall be brought in as a trustee. Then majority vote will control; an absolute, permanent impasse is most remote. If one should develop, the trustees may join in asking a probate court for instructions, a far better route than litigation between mother and children. The bank will have a fiduciary duty to the children as second beneficiaries as well as to the widow, the primary beneficiary.

The will might instruct that upon the death of either child, the bank would be joined as a trustee. Upon the death of the mother, the trust would terminate and the estate be distributed to the two children or their issue, unless continued for the purpose of educating testator's grandchildren.

The likelihood is that such a trust would accomplish its purposes without going outside the family for a trustee. But it would have the stability of a bank ready in the background.

As remarked when discussing

executors, if the estate includes a heavy investment in a going concern, thought should be given to securing the best practical advice available for that particular enterprise. A partner or fellow shareholder will have a common interest in wanting the concern to prosper and should know how best to dispose of it. On the other hand, if the value of the share of the estate has not been fixed by a buy-out agreement, a surviving partner or shareholder may have an adverse interest. Economic motivation might be to buy at a bargain.

Another factor deserving careful thought when choosing the trustee is his (or her, their, or its) discretionary responsibilities in relation to beneficiaries. There is an inherent conflict of interest between generations and, often, between individual beneficiaries. Is the proposed trustee trained or sufficiently wise, without prior experience as a trustee, to determine between adverse interests? Shall available funds be invested in growth stocks with low current yield, obviously to the benefit of the second generation, as against bonds, with maximum safe income to the first beneficiaries? How much shall be drawn against principal for this purpose or that? During the life of a long trust, many policy questions must be determined which never reach the desk of an executor. So the natural and best choice as executor might not be the best prospect for trustee.

When for the first time you are considering establishing a trust, whether testamentary or *inter vivos,* you will be searching for the answer to twin questions: (1) Shall I have a trust? (2) If I do, who shall be my trustee? It seems efficient to bring into this chapter on "who" a discussion of a problem which is also related to your study of "shall I?" It is the conflict of interest faced by advisers of consequence — the bank's trust officers.

The trust officer will in good faith believe he is objective as he views your problems. He will give you his honest recommendations. But he is on the payroll of a corporate trustee. Securing new business is part of his work.

So, in response to your question, "Is a trust advisable?" a professional trust officer may be inclined to reply "Yes," unless the answer is most obviously "No."

Your next query is "Who should be my trustee? Shall I name my younger brother and son as trustees, or designate a bank?" The trust officer may feel compelled to say, "A bank is better," even though you have two qualified people in your own family.

You divert a bit and inquire about executors. The banker naturally discusses the advantages of continuity in postmortem management and recommends the bank as executor in preference to your brother and your son. When you ask "Which bank?" is he going to recommend a competitor even though, in fact, a rival bank may be better situated to handle your affairs? Suppose the competitor bank has a major branch in the midst of the wheat country where your three-generation family ranch (your principal asset) is located, while your friendly adviser's bank does not happen to have a branch within 200 miles of your barns.

And if you ask whether your life insurance funds should be paid into the trust to be administered by the bank or left with Provident Mutual to be paid out in monthly installments, will the banker not point to the greater flexibility of the trust at the bank and refrain from adducing arguments which might convince you that, in your situation, insurance funds should be left with the insurance company?

As already indicated, a bank has advantages not possessed by individuals. Presumably immortal, it does not move to another city. The trust work is done by specialists in investments and other fields. Their procedures are audited by accountants, then by state or federal bank examiners. There is no occasion for the testator to fear that the trustee might abscond with negotiable trust assets in his portmanteau.

Contrary to literature's traditional banker image, the trust officers are mostly sympathetic, interested in doing the best possible job for each beneficiary. Indeed they must. The bank spends thousands of dollars touting the virtues of its trust department. One unhappy widow at one dinner party can undo $10,000 worth of advertising. As a matter of economic survival, the trust officers must be good to beneficiaries. Often their patience goes far beyond the call of duty; usually no relative could be more considerate of an impossible beneficiary unable to comprehend the simplest business problem.

There is an incidental aspect when deciding which bank to name. The inclination is to use the bank where a friend or someone especially personable works. The test should be: (1) Is this a sound bank, with a trust department of high repute? (2) Has it know-how in the type of assets which will comprise the bulk of my estate? (3) Is it a bank where my family and I feel at home? Do not tie to one or two individuals. The older of them will shortly retire and the younger may leave for a better job elsewhere.

In the discussion of the possible slant of bank officers, there was not a scintilla of inference that other prospective fiduciaries are not also subject to economic and personal tugs. The potential dilemma of a former partner if serving as executor or trustee has been mentioned. When you are deliberating concerning the wisdom of selecting any individual (except the evident natural choice) as your personal representative, a substantial tenet may be involved: Do not choose the person who pushes herself or himself forward — the one who volunteers.

It is in order for the bank to rent billboards enticing all who read to utilize its trust services. It is quite another matter when any individual, including your lawyer, insinuates himself into the position of executor or trustee of your estate. If he is the right choice, that idea will have occurred to you or to one of your advisers without any hint from him.

Often the best formula is to appoint the friend and the bank as cotrustees, with the bank obliged to acquiesce in certain types of business decisions by the friend, without liability on the part of the bank for mistakes made in reliance on the friend. Testator would be prudent to review proposed fee arrangements between them.

No, there was no inference that bank trust officers are more susceptible to conflicts in economic interest than are other people. Indeed, since most of them have tenure and retirement pay, they would seem better insulated from economic pressure than are ordinary mortals.

Not infrequently, testator's lawyer is asked to serve as executor or trustee, sometimes as cotrustee. There are more than a few situations where this continuing representation is highly advantageous to the estate and to its beneficiaries. Possibly also to creditors when a complicated estate is marginal. If there has been a long and intimate professional relationship, it may seem the lawyer's duty to the family to accept. But the fee formula should be agreed upon directly with testator, in writing, and not left to negotiations with kinfolk stunned by shock. And, I believe, the assumption should be *against* the lawyer's serving in any other than his or her legal capacity.

Many lawyers would challenge that assumption — and, *in their environment,* rightly so. An eminent lawyer, a veteran in the fields of estates and trusts, writes: "I take strong issue with you on your recommendation against the appointment of a lawyer as fiduciary." He asserts: "Where an inexperienced layman is named as executor or trustee, the lawyer does virtually all the work anyway. Granted lawyers "are not qualified to give investment advice, neither is anybody else." The institution fiduciary does an excellent job of record keeping. But its "biggest advantage is continuity and absolute security, not to be despised. However, the continuity aspect is diluted by constantly changing personnel. New employees cannot be expected to perpetuate an intimate personal relationship."

He concludes: "For most estates a good

lawyer who has the confidence of the family is the most desirable of fiduciaries. However, for an estate of real magnitude and long duration, a bank is probably preferable.''

I concede great validity in his viewpoint when testator is represented by an established legal firm (1) which enjoys an impeccable record in business and trust affairs, and (2) whose office is structured to handle the mechanics of estate and trust matters. Particularly in the older cities, there are such firms, some counting back several generations. (Ideally, in a back room, there would be a little old man in shirtsleeves, with a quill pen, keeping trust records in a big book at a standup desk.) A prudent testator might well prefer their expertise to that of the trust officers of a bank.

So I go along with use of lawyers as fiduciaries in the right environment. But I adhere to my point that, generally speaking, the lawyer should concentrate on being an attorney and advise and watch the other fiduciaries.

When discussing guardians, a heresy

was proposed to the effect that often it is better to refrain from enlisting the guardian in advance. The reverse is true with executors; there may be duties to perform within hours of death. The proposed trustee should also know about the trust. If an individual, you should not surprise him or her; your choice might not wish to serve and decline to act. A trustee bank wants business, but not certain types of business. It will often accept a small, unprofitable trust as a matter of public relations, but should not have one thrust upon it without an advance conference and acquiescence.

## ON CHANGING TRUSTEES

What college sophomore likes to be told he cannot afford a car or what widow enjoys being admonished that she must spend less and cannot employ an interior decorator to refurbish the living and dining rooms?

The thought at once occurs: Who was really at fault? The widow? Or a trust officer who failed to keep her fully informed about the cash requirements of the trust in relation to income? If asked, the trust officer would respond that she has been sent quarterly statements produced by a data processing machine.

The widow might have a burning answer to that: "Those things? No one can understand them. I don't know one woman who knows what they mean."

Here we have an unfortunate lack of liaison. Perhaps actually it was an exceedingly well-run trust with an excellent investment record.

Or perhaps the trustee, institutional or individual, was not doing an acceptable job. Should the trustee be unassailable in its position or should the beneficiaries be allowed to change trustees, at least once or twice? If so, (1) without giving reasons? (2) After stating reasons?

The testator may be fully aware of his wife's tendency to spend excessively and does not foresee sound financial judgment in the children for many years to come. He gives an emphatic "No" to any right to change. The point is the *right* of irked beneficiaries to change. If there are provable violations of the exalted fiduciary standards of the trusteeship, the court will change trustees.

But if the testator (the donor, the trustor) favors a right to change, it should be exercisable without reason. Just as you may change doctor or lawyer or gingerbread man. If reasons are required, they invite charges, countercharges, recriminations, and possible litigation. A paragraph like this will make change possible:

Legally competent beneficiaries to whom more than fifty percent of the income of this trust is distributable by the trustee, whether obligatory or at the discretion of the trustee, by written notice may remove any corporate trustee named and appoint as successor corporate trustee any bank authorized to perform trust services in the state of Ohio with a net worth or capital in excess of $5,000,000.

Then follow simple provisions regarding notices and windup accounting.

*Caveat to beneficiaries:* Do not hastily divorce your trustee. Make sure there is a deep and incurable fault on its part, and not merely a curable failure in communication or a personality problem. You may soon decide your new trustee has the same faults, perhaps worse or more. Your first trustee will not welcome you back and the third eligible bank develops plausible reasons for not accepting you. So be sure before you shift. After all, you may be in *pari delicto,* which is a lawyer's way of saying "partly to blame."

The caveat is not to say I disapprove the provision. The opposite is true. I favor it, except when trustor (the testator) believes there are good reasons for not granting particular beneficiaries so much power.

## YOUR LAWYER

Your lawyer has a high fiduciary duty in his every relationship with you. He often speaks for you. He is your very first fiduciary in the sequence of will, death, administration, and distribution of your estate. What are the criteria when choosing this person?

Until recently, the lawyers have made it very hard for you. Most have not frankly faced the reality that not everyone can do everything. In the days of Abe Lincoln, the lawyer was an all-purpose adviser and warrior; that tradition has continued. The medical profession, some think, has swung too far into specialization — does the doctor treat the left ear as well as the right? During recent years lawyers have been making progress toward a well-balanced recognition of compartmentalized expertise.

If fortunate, the testator has his or her own lawyer or legal firm whose abilities in estate planning cannot be doubted. Either one is already familiar with testator's affairs. That is the ideal. The next most desirable route is available if you already know a seasoned lawyer in whose integrity and ability you have complete confidence. If you have correctly assessed your adviser, you will be frankly told whether estate planning is within the special skills of that office. If not, other counsel will be recommended to you.

The question here is: How does a stranger find a lawyer highly competent in the planning and drafting of wills? The succinct answer is: Ask of those who should know. Secure and compare two or three or more answers. Ask a trust officer at one or more banks for several suggestions. He will tell you which lawyer represents the bank so you can avoid a conflict of interest if you think there may be one. Ask a businessman whom you admire. If you know one well enough to do so, ask the executor of an estate in the midst of probate. Ask a lawyer who is known to accept only criminal or tort (accident) or patent cases.

Those lucky enough to live in a village or on a farm may have to drive to the county seat or to ''the city'' to have a sufficient breadth of choice. It may be well worth it.

Do not choose a lawyer in whom you do not have fullest confidence — in his or her character, training, and know-how in relation to the complexities of your estate and family. When you have chosen wisely, your lawyer may be of great assistance as you are selecting your executor, trustee, and guardian.

There are instances ranging from irritation to tragedy where decedent's executor, although disapproving the choice, feels obligated to retain the lawyer who drew the will as attorney for the estate. Unless there is a binding agreement between testator and the lawyer, that is not so. An indication of preference in the will may or may not demonstrate an agreement. Generally the personal representative of decedent may choose counsel for the estate.

Customarily, when a bank is named as executor, it selects the draftsman of the will as attorney for the estate. That is natural; this person was testator's own choice. But should the family be unhappy with the selection, the trust officers will listen to the objections. If the lawyer and the beneficiaries are not mutually *simpatico,* a rocky road stretches ahead of all concerned with that estate.

## SEVEN

# Trusts

A "trust" is the holding of property, real or personal, for the benefit of the person or persons or institutions for whom the trust was created.

Rivaling the corporate concept in importance, the development of the rules pertaining to trusts is sometimes referred to as one of the most significant achievements of Anglo-American law. A one-volume law dictionary includes nearly fifty subheadings in bold black type under the word "trust"; it does not purport to be complete. The ancient juridical concept called a trust is often an important, sometimes the only, legal tool available to testators as they and their advisers chart the family course.

# DEFINITIONS

The person who establishes the trust is called "trustor," "grantor," "settlor," or "donor." If the trust is established by a will, he is the "testator." The "trustee" is the person or institution (a bank or trust company) designated by the trustor or testator or appointed by the court to administer the trust.

Recipients of the benefits of the trust are the "beneficiaries." The interest of a "contingent beneficiary" is dependent upon some future, uncertain event.

An *inter vivos* or "living" trust is established during the lifetime of the trustor. A trust may be for the benefit of the person who establishes it or for the benefit of others. Occasionally the trustor chooses to serve as the trustee, or as one of them, and also as the beneficiary, or as one of them. Such a dual or treble relationship should not be undertaken except for good reasons, upon the advice of an attorney especially skilled in trust matters. For example, if a testator establishes a trust for his grandchildren and names himself as trustee with vaguely worded powers to tap trust principal for their benefit the trust fund may end as a part of the testator's estate. The powers of the trustor-trustee (testator) must be limited by an ascertainable standard, preferably strict.

A living trust becomes a reality when the person who creates the trust and the trustee sign the trust agreement — often called a "deed of trust" or "trust indenture" — and the trustor conveys securities, real estate, or other property to the trustee to be administered and distributed according to his instructions.

A "testamentary trust" is established by a testator in a will. It comes into being when the executors of the estate distribute assets to the trustee or trustees named in the will or appointed by the court if the named trustee is unable to act.

One who will enjoy trust income for life may be said to have a "life tenancy"; there is a "life tenant" or, more exactly, a "life income beneficiary." Those who follow as beneficiaries are "remaindermen." A "contingent" trust does itself not become operative until the happening of a named future event.

The property owned in trust by the trustee and being administered as instructed in the trust indenture is variously referred to as the "trust fund," or "principal," or *corpus* (the body), or *res* (thing).

A trust, whether living or testamentary, may be in whole or in part "charitable" (see Glossary). Charitable or public trusts are established to assist a charitable institution or the public generally, rather than for the benefit of named individuals and their successors. If the charitable aspect is to come into being after the death of a primary beneficiary, the tax benefit of the "charitable remainder" may be lost or radically diminished unless that portion of the trust be drafted with exquisite care.

It is the function of the testator-trustor formulating the estate plan to determine the objectives of the trust. The apparatus of the trust and the legal description of testator's objectives should be spelled out by someone sophisticated in trust affairs. State laws differ, but fundamental trust concepts have persisted for many years.

## THE THRESHOLD QUESTION

The initial question is, under what circumstances should an estate planner give serious consideration to the utilization of a trust, whether *inter vivos,* to be effective during trustor's lifetime, or testamentary? The indicators are as varied as are the pigeonholes into which family circumstances may be sorted. Some are crystal-clear "Negative." Others signal an imperative "Affirmative." The bulk are in between, with gradations in the force of varying factors. In one framework of circumstances, for example, marriage of a child points strongly trustward, yet in a different framework, it makes a trust seem superfluous.

Factors march before the mind of testator-trustor, each to be given the weight it deserves in that particular family and economic structure. They include:

1. Testator's own age, physical health, and mental prognosis. Is a living trust indicated to protect himself and thus protect his family?

2. Are the assets such that an *inter vivos* (living) trust should be used as part of the process of preparing for postmortem management, as prescribed in Chapters 9 and 11?

3. Does any beneficiary need the protection of a testamentary trust — in respect to investment of principal? In respect to optional expenditures of income? In respect to drafts on principal for specified purposes? Does a softhearted beneficiary need insulation from collateral relatives and solicitors for charities?

When the testator-trustor weighs the responses to these questions, the personalities of, and personal factors surrounding, each beneficiary come to the fore. Age? Health? Marital status?

167

Vocation? Available to manage properties, or itinerant?

4. Will a testamentary trust make possible significant tax savings on the second death, as described in Chapter 13? Or will an irrevocable living trust be a medium for saving taxes on the first? (Chapter 12, page 364.)

5. Do I want a long-term program, perhaps for great-grandchildren or a charity?

6. My assets stemmed from the sale of the family farm; or my assets derived from the sale of the machine shop which I built up and operated for forty years. What do I know about investments?

The ulitmate answer is not nearly so elusive as the questionnaire may seem to imply. As already indicated, a positive answer to even one question, certainly to two or three, may bring a conclusive overall answer, "Yes, I should create a trust" or "No, no trust for me." For example: The lone factor of a taxable estate of upward of $200,000 usually leads to the conclusion that the tax-saving possibilities of a trust cannot be ignored.

## LIVING TRUSTS

Planning for *premortem* management may be as important a part of overall estate planning as is planning for the *post*mortem management, elaborated in Chapters 9 and 11. Indeed, they overlap to a considerable degree.

By *"pre*mortem planning" I mean provision for that vacillating, uncertain twilight phase in business acumen which comes upon many who live into a period of senility without a legal adjudication of incompetency. A critical aspect is: If the trustor and his or her family are to enjoy the benefits and sense of security which come with an *inter vivos* trust, it *must* be executed at least one day before it *has* to be executed. And who can forecast exactly the swiftness of degeneration of mental and physical health? More than once my advice has been ignored when I have recommended — urged — that a client set up the legal mechanism designed to manage things material and provide for medical, nursing, and related care, beginning the very morning when trustor can no longer make decisions, sign checks, deposit coupons, and do the other things necessary to a self-sufficient economic life. "I still know what I am doing. I can walk to the bank. I would be lost without these things to do," the client responds.

Then suddenly the oldster is no longer competent; it is too late to sign a trust instrument. There is need for a court guardianship. The legal wheels turn well enough. But they are costly when compared with a living trust, not so efficient, and sometimes humiliating to the ward and to kinfolk.

The closest timing I have seen was that of a man just past eighty. He seemed so alert that, while I had told him of the functioning of living trusts, I had not pressed him to authorize one. Early on a Monday morning he came in and said: "It is time for me to have a receiver. You are it." "Receiver" is an apt word meaning a person appointed to handle the properties of another, usually incident to litigation. His was an unusual but excellent use of the term. I replied: "I will not be your receiver. I will be your watchman and help your trustee bank do a superlative job for you and the family. A revocable *inter vivos* trust will be ready for signing tomorrow." I had a distinct feeling that his document should be given emergency priority; that over the weekend an internal clock had warned him. The next afternoon, fully competent, he signed the trust indenture.

A fortnight later he suffered a stroke and became incapable of handling business transactions. For nearly three years he lived on. No one had to go to court. Every care and comfort were made available to him and his wife, who could not possibly have handled the simplest business affair (which was perhaps his fault). Such a use is, I believe, one of the highest functions of the legal concept called a living trust.

## Revocable and irrevocable trusts

During lifetime, trusts divide into those which are revocable and those which are irrevocable. A revocable trust is one that can be amended or terminated by the person who created it. An irrevocable trust is one that cannot be changed or canceled. Each has useful functions, quite different in character.

Most living trusts are revocable at any time. If revocable, there is no gift tax, as there may be incident to an irrevocable trust. No gift tax having been paid on the conveyance to the revocable trust, there is no saving in taxes amerced because of the passage of the property by death.

Inherent in the revocable trust is the right of trustor to withdraw or add properties, to change beneficiaries or allocations to them, to change trustees — in fact, to do anything he or she pleases, subject always to the right of the trustee to withdraw if it does not wish to serve under changed conditions.

The authority accorded the trustee under a revocable living trust ranges from absolute (until modified or revoked) to minimal. The trustor may say:

> Here is my portfolio. Until I revoke this trust or instruct you otherwise, invest and reinvest as you deem a prudent man would, sending me the net income.

Then he or she may travel and pay no attention to business affairs. Many people have found that to be able to do this is reason enough for the trust.

Or trustors may impose guidelines and alter them as they see fit. They may require that proposed changes in portfolio be submitted to them for approval. Indeed, custodial arrangements which, in practical effect, reach about the same result as some revocable trusts go by the name of "management account," "custodial trust," "agency account" or "safekeeping account." But such a program lacks the all-important authority to the trustee to care for the trustor — to pay bills and in general to carry on should need arise.

A revocable trust cannot be made "fail-safe." If the trustor-testator wants absolute assurance that from the day of signing to day of death the trustee will handle business affairs, the route of the irrevocable trust must be elected while trustor is still clearly competent.

A revocable trust is subject to the hazard that just when it is needed most, the trustor-beneficiary becomes mentally muddled, revokes the trust, and demands the return of all properties in the possession of the trustee. Then a formal court guardianship may be the only solution. Presumably the required proceedings would be started by next of kin.

In the first sentence of the preceding paragraph, I nearly said "theoretical hazard" instead of "hazard" because almost always the trustor-beneficiary and the family are thankful that the trust is there. They want it to last out the life of the trustor-beneficiary without any legal challenge. However, if trustor has no more than granted an agency to establish a trust and if the validity of the agency is contested in court, it will be questionable whether the property of an incompetent can be taken over or held on the basis of a prior revocable authority. A fundamental rule is to the effect that death or incompetency terminates an agency. A revocable trust is akin to an agency.

The inclusion of trust provisions in a will is not the equivalent of establishing an *inter vivos* trust. Instead, it might be termed a potential trust — contingent upon the death of testator. Death brings the moment of finality; an irrevocable trust has been created. No longer is the will ambulatory, subject to change and revocation.

Similarly, when a trustor completes a valid, irrevocable *inter vivos* trust, the act is final, of course subject to the postmortem type of flexibility provisions which are the target of Chapter 5. The property (subject to the value of reserved income, if any) is no longer part of trustor's estate. As already stated, gift taxes may become payable when the trust is established. Unless later, after death, taxing authorities successfully assert that the conveyance to the trustee was a gift in contemplation of death (or claim some other defect such as a reservation of too broad or too many powers by the donor), the property of the trust remains foreign to trustor's other properties and when death comes is not part of the taxable estate. Certainly no one should execute an irrevocable *inter vivos* trust without having given due heed to the conclusiveness of this act and its legal consequences.

Some wills direct that named assets or all the residuary estate pass into an already-established irrevocable trust or to a revocable living trust which carries the directive of the trustor-testator that it continue after death. Adding estate assets to a trust is often called "pouring over." A will which so directs may be called a "pour-over will."

### Standby and take-over trusts

Many a venerable gentleman with a well-planned will has reached a point in physical and mental health where he should protect his estate for his own sake.

Yet he cannot quite bring himself to sign away the powers of a lifetime to a trustee, even under a revocable trust. I have observed that women are often equally reluctant in respect to their properties, whether recently willed them directly by a now-deceased husband or derived from the widow's own family. A standby or take-over program — a halfway trust — may break the impasse.

There are three principal types of halfway trusts: (1) a completed token standby trust, with formulas for adding assets; (2) a trust wherein the trustor is also the trustee and the primary, but not the only, beneficiary; and (3) a custodial arrangement. Each is subject to variations. Many attorneys may prefer a different method of safeguarding the client of waning abilities who is adamant in refusing to execute a conventional *inter vivos* trust to protect personal and property interests, even though walking alone with no family backing. "Conventional" means a present transfer of trust assets to a trustee other than trustor pursuant to a written trust agreement.

1. *Standby Trusts:* By "standby" I mean a completed trust but one without much in it. Perhaps $1,000; perhaps $5,000 or $10,000. The trustee should have at least a token. Trustor is authorized to add assets. If and when the trustor requests that it do so or need arises, the trustee will take over all, or the designated portions of, trustor's properties.

The trust instrument provides the formula. It might read something like this:

If Dr. Robert R. Robinson, Trustor's physician, or any other doctor of medicine consulted by Trustor advises the bank, in writing, that in his opinion Trustor has become physically or mentally inadequate when making business decisions and should not be managing fiscal affairs, the Trustee shall take possession of all the assets named or referred to in Article I hereof (including the opening of the safe-deposit box) not already in the hands of the Trustee. If, for any reason, the Trustee should have doubt as to the soundness of the opinion from Dr. Robinson, or other physician, it may, at the expense of Trustor, require an examination and confirmatory advice from a consulting physician.

An inventory of all the assets eventually to be included in the trust would be set forth either in the body of the trust instrument or by listing in an exhibit attached thereto.

Other provisions of the trust would grant trustee wide latitude in expending funds for the care and comfort of the trustor-beneficiary. The language used must of course be tuned to the magnitude of the trust estate. A $100,000 trust cannot be expected to supply the luxuries of a $1,000,000 trust.

A major problem is to find a bank which will commit itself to such a trust agreement. Some will, but most banks are reluctant to take over the properties of such a sick customer without court approval, which may be difficult to obtain if mental competence is actually in question.

**2.** *Trustor as Sole Trustee:* As part of the definition of *inter vivos* trusts near the beginning of this chapter, it is recited that occasionally the trustor names himself or herself as trustee, or as one of them, and also as the first beneficiary. This device also may be used to cut the Gordian knot when there should be a trust, whether revocable or irrevocable, but the trustor cannot take the step to give up custody or control of the investment portfolio and other business affairs, although recognizing that suddenly, perhaps soon, the protection of a trust may be desperately needed. So, reluctantly, the trustor becomes also first trustee as well as beneficiary, naming the bank as successor trustee to take over when requested to do so by the trustor-trustee-beneficiary or upon certification by a physician, as already described. Here the bank is on firmer ground. It is taking over the assets of an already-established trust from a trustee, in contrast to absorbing assets of a sick person into a token trust.

However, it will be surprising if a

trustee bank will unequivocally agree to take over as successor trustee without satisfying itself as to the assets, the records kept by the first named trustee and the operation and conduct of trust affairs. The great hazard is that a trustor-trustee-beneficiary may continue *as trustee* longer than able to do so and that the trust may be in sorry shape — unacceptable to a careful corporate trustee whose standards may well require a set of books established by a skilled accountant and faithfully maintained by a competent bookkeeper.

Before me is a printed form used by a bank. The first sentence says:

I, John Doe, transfer, convey, and set over the following assets unto myself as Trustee. . . .

Then follows a listing of properties and provisions enabling the bank to function as trustee.

When the trust is first executed by John Doe, the bank will sign a paragraph on the last page entitled ''Conditional

181

Acquiescence in Trust," which commits the bank to take over if (and only if) the trust affairs are in good order. Before Abraham Stoner (our proposed trustor-trustee-beneficiary) causes registered securities to be transferred into the name of "Abraham Stoner Trust" or "Abraham Stoner, trustee," he should make sure that his broker or bank will guarantee his transfer *as trustee* to the end that it may not be necessary to send the trust document to a meticulous transfer agent to demonstrate Stoner's authority as trustee. Assuming such a commitment by the bank or reliable broker, this is the desirable route.

If refusal by both bank and broker should create a roadblock, perhaps Stoner's attorney and the successor trustee will agree that the simpler method is to continue to register the securities in the name "Abraham Stoner" and lodge them in a special envelope in his box at the bank, leaving it to the trust document to confirm which of his papers are within the trust. If the trustor-trustee proves to be a faithful and careful trustee, this simple formula should work out well. If not, it may end in a guardianship of Stoner.

3. *Custodial Arrangements:* A closer step toward a fully established trust, whether revocable or irrevocable, is the custodial type of arrangement with the trustee, usually a bank, though I have seen it operate successfully with mature children as trustees. Until the happening of a take-over event, the duties of the trustee are limited to registration, safekeeping, bookkeeping, and related incidentals. Trustor retains all investment responsibilities. The custodial fee is perhaps half (or even less) the usual fee for a trustee.

But the person who is determined to carry on independently to the very end of life may be unable to tolerate surrendering possession of his or her assets to a third-party custodian or agent. Nor can this person see value received for the custodial fee which will be charged for the service.

Having considered three types of transitory or take-over devices — halfway trusts — we should close by making the following statements:

This discussion does not imply that most people need think in terms of an immediate *inter vivos* trust, or of one of the three halfway measures just described. Competent members of the family may be available to carry on informally during most emergencies, even though prolonged. But every oldster should be aware of the possibilities and give them careful consideration while still competent. I know of lawyers who have obstinately refused to enter into an *inter vivos* program for themselves and have spent their closing years under the cloud of a court guardianship.

Under the heading "The Threshold Question" earlier in this chapter, criteria are given for consideration when deciding whether you should create a trust. If you should determine that a living trust is indicated, usually a carefully tailored, completed (not halfway) revocable trust is the best medium. Once executed and in operation, the trust will rarely be revoked and the advantages which impelled you to sign it be lost. Nevertheless, if sound judgment impels revocation or amendment of the trust, the door is not locked.

One must recognize that there are situations where a person wants even less than a halfway trust. A *power of attorney* may be the answer. It is a document by which an individual appoints another his "true and lawful" attorney (often called attorney-in-fact) to act in his place and stead. A *general* power gives the attorney broad latitude in acting for the principal. A *special* power limits the authority to a specified act or to enumerated acts or to a limited type of act. Grandmother may authorize grandson Gilbert to draw on specified bank accounts for the payment of her living, medical, and hospital expenses, with no authority to tamper with investments. An ailing husband may constitute his wife his attorney-in-fact to handle all business affairs.

Traditionally, a power of attorney terminates with the death or incompetency of the grantor unless, as the law puts it, "it is coupled with an interest." Delving into that legal concept would be a digression; joint ownership of property would be one example.

Some statutes now permit a power of attorney (1) to survive incompetency but not (as far as I know) death, or (2) to become effective upon the disability of the principal, the grantor of the power. It can be a useful tool for people who want the minimum in management of their affairs by others. Like a revocable *inter vivos* trust, it can always be amended or revoked. I personally favor a limited or special power unless it is manifest that the attorney-in-fact should have very broad powers. This notion is predicated on personal as well as legal reasons. Grandmother may be restive if her grandson has almost unlimited powers, even though he is a competent fellow, diligent, and of undoubted integrity.

## Clifford trusts

The law has a duty to provide processes and legal (not economic) protection for the accomplishment of every socially desirable objective. There is need for trusts which:

Relieve trustor of the burden of paying taxes measured by income flowing from trust assets, and
Permit trustor to take back the assets of the trust when it has served its purpose.

In response, the law developed the Clifford Trust. Its demands are not onerous.

1. The duration of the trust must be for the life of the beneficiary, or
2. For at least ten years and a day.
3. Its purpose must be other than fulfilling a legal obligation of the trustor.
4. It must be a bona fide trust, trustor giving up domain over his or her property for the period of the trust.

If these requirements are met, income from trust properties will be taxed to the beneficiary of the trust, not to trustor.

Suppose the prospective trustor to be a professional man in his peak earning years. He has children in high school and college; two look forward to professional school. For at least a decade his will be a very expensive family. He also has a mother and a mother-in-law, each lacking income beyond social security. He has been subsidizing them. Both look as though they have a fair life expectancy.

He has a well-selected investment portfolio worth about $200,000, yielding $10,000 a year. His professional income puts him into the 60 percent tax bracket. So this pleasant unearned income of $10,000 shrinks to less than $5,000 spendable dollars. Because of inflation, he does not want his savings in tax-exempt bonds. He must consume all his investment income and tap his earned income by approximately $1,500 a year if he is to subsidize each mother $250 a month, as he and his wife wish to continue to do.

He becomes a trustor and establishes two Clifford Trusts. His brother is trustee, with a bank as successor — a nonprofit, public relations assignment to the bank if it ever takes over. To each trust is conveyed one-half trustor's securities, yielding about $5,000 each. Subject to taxes at a low rate, each mother will receive about $500 a month and be able to live more nearly as trustor thinks a grandmother of his children should live.

The trust properties are to be returned to trustor upon the death of a grandmother.

Without clear approval of counsel, parents should not count on a Clifford Trust to finance the education of their own children. (That is an excellent project for grandparents and uncles and aunts who have no legal obligation to the youngsters.) What is a parent's legal obligation in respect to education of children? Private schools in preference to public schools? Dancing lessons? Music lessons? A South Carolina lawyer established a trust which paid for these luxuries. A trial judge of the U.S. Court of Claims held that the father was not required to provide deluxe schools and coaching for his children nor had he contracted to do so. His trust was upheld.

A Clifford Trust may provide dollars for a dismissed mistress, or for friends, or for a charity as it embarks upon a pilot program.

### Totten trusts

The Totten Trust is a convenient and simple medium for making tentative financial provision for limited objectives, such as schooling for the young or care for the aged. It is created by the deposit of funds in a bank by a person in his or her own name as trustee for another, as father or mother for son. The depositor, say the father, may withdraw all or any part of the account whenever he decides to do so. If upon his death there is a balance, it passes to the son, even though the will leaves "all my property to my wife."

A Totten Trust is not a true trust; it is tentative, provisional. Why bother, you ask? When depositor wishes to help the son, he can as easily draw on his usual checking account and can provide for the boy in his will. True. But sometimes people wish to segregate funds for a certain purpose subject to change of mind. Today, let us say, the prospective Totten Trustor has ample funds. Today he is willing to set aside $10,000 for a specified purpose. But as long as he lives, he wishes to do the deciding in respect to drafts upon the fund. He wants to be able to retrieve the balance if the fund is not consumed. Yet, if he should die, he wants the beneficiary to own the unused portion.

I see expensive advertisements extolling Christmas savings accounts. So I assume there must be many of them. There is, I think, an analogy. I would suppose that the Christmas savers would find it simpler to budget and save through the usual channels. But they and the Totten Trustor find the earmarking useful. The latter would point out that the opening of this specialized bank account is simpler than drafting a codicil to a will and is subject to day-to-day control (by deposit or drafts) without consulting anyone.

During his lifetime the depositor — the father, for example — may of course complete the gift by unequivocal acts such as delivery of the passbook, authorizing the beneficiary to withdraw funds, and assignment of the account. If large enough, a gift tax would be triggered. Unless there is a completed gift, the balance in the account at depositor's death is taxed in his estate. While he lives, interest received from the deposit is part of his income on which he must pay income taxes.

## GENERAL POWERS OF TRUSTEE

It is not unusual to speak of the "general powers" of the trustee in contrast to "special instructions" to the trustee. "General powers" include the broad authorizations which enable the trustee to hold legal title to manage and deal in testator's properties on behalf of the beneficiaries, as though the trustee were the owner.

The "special instructions" are your directives which adapt the trust to your estate and family.

General powers may be delineated in great detail, taking as much as three or four pages, single-spaced, in the will or trust indenture. The middle route is an adequate but abbreviated form. Or, in many states, the "general powers" may be read into the document by reference to the laws of the state wherein the trustor-testator resides. The language might be similar to the following:

In all matters affecting this trust:

(a) The trustee shall exercise the judgment which prudent, discreet, and intelligent men exercise in the management of their own affairs in regard to the permanent disposition of their funds considering both probable income and safety of their capital.

(b) The trustee shall have the general

powers set forth in Chapter —— of the Laws of the State of —————— and amendments thereto, if any there should be, not substantially changing the intent and purposes of those chapters as enacted.

I prefer the middle route — describing the powers in the trust instrument in language sufficient but not verbose. As the testator-trustor, you may want to know what you are signing and will not be content with a reference to a statute. The general powers may be spelled out in an exhibit attached to the will, thus avoiding an interruption to the flow of your instructions as testator.

You may of course limit the general powers of the trustee; you need not permit him "to deal with your property as though it were his own." Then you must consider whether you are needlessly handicapping your own fiduciary in the management of your affairs.

## SOME SPECIAL INSTRUCTIONS TO TRUSTEE

In nearly every chapter of this book can be found references to provisions which might be classified as special instructions to the trustees. Indeed, the will as a whole may be thought of as final orders from the commander of this estate on permanent assignment to duties elsewhere. Commands to the executors, to the trustees if any, to the beneficiaries, and, subject to the laws of the land, to the probate court.

For but two examples: the important possible special instructions in respect to sprinkling and accumulation trusts were touched upon in Chapter 5 (pages 119 to 121) when considering ways and means of attaining flexibility in decision making after death.

Here we advert to selected special instructions which, in one form or another, appear in many trusts in respect to (1) investments; (2) things; (3)

protective trusts; (4) income and care of beneficiaries and — the climax — the ultimate distribution of the principal of the trust estate.

## *Investments*

If the bulk of your estate will be in securities, savings accounts, and other investment items, it is likely that the only *investment* instruction you will wish to give your trustee is to follow the "prudent man" rule. In the preceding section, it is stated in condensed form. It contrasts sharply with a legal list approach; that is, to tell your trustee to invest only in bonds of such and such a rating and in stocks of clearly investment quality. A legal list excludes real estate, although a wise and prudent investor might deem a certain equity in real estate ideal for your trust.

If, however, your estate will probably include a going business, or a farm, or real estate, you may wish to give what you deem to be sage instructions in respect to operations or liquidation. Often your instructions can be supplemented by authorizing the trustee to rely on the advice of someone in whom you have great confidence. If, for example, your portfolio includes a block of stock in a family or other close corporation, you may instruct that none may be sold without the written approval of brother Fred or sister Florence.

The variations in possible sensible special instructions in respect to investments are as great as the differences between varied holdings. But, as you instruct, always remember this: You cannot foretell all problems which will face your trustee. If you have chosen well, the trustee should have wide latitude in meeting changing conditions.

## Things

In respect to tangibles — things — your underlying instruction to the executor is whether a particular item (or class of items) not specifically bequeathed to someone is (1) to be sold or to pass to the trust; and (2) if sold, where the proceeds are to go, or if there is a direction against sale of the item, what is to be done with it. Most unlisted things are of course caught up in a comprehensive paragraph concerning "all furniture, furnishings, and other usables." Chapter 4 contains a number of suggestions concerning handling of things, from a poem to a pet.

As testator-trustor, you have the power to tell what shall be done with your one rare painting or the grandfather's clock which has been in the family for five generations. Instead of making specific bequests to be distributed by your executor, you may pass unique items to your trustee to be distributed on the happening of a specified event, such as your silverware to your two granddaughters, one-half to each when she marries or reaches twenty-two years of age.

## Protective trusts

It is hard to think of a trust which, in a sense, is not a protective trust. What special financial protection can be given trustor's beneficiaries against their own acts, including the trustor as a beneficiary? A testator, perhaps the *pater familias* with inherited wealth, might himself have an alcohol problem, or for other reasons be the greatest hazard to his own loved ones. He could make completed irrevocable gifts if he were so inclined, divesting himself of all but Buddha's begging bowl. He seldom does.

Can he establish an irrevocable trust with himself as one of the income beneficiaries, containing a strong spendthrift clause (introduced in Chapter 4, page 91) which will protect the trust against his own creditors and against his own transfers of *his* interest as a beneficiary under the trust? Certainly not, if he names himself as trustee. And the almost-universal rule is that he cannot thus protect himself (and through him the family) even though a third-party trustee is named. It would be an excellent estate-planning tool if one could; wealthy, spendthrift parents and grandparents are not unknown. Neither is the old gentleman isolated by a buxom nurse.

But most courts enforce provisions of the spendthrift type when the trust is established by someone other than the protected person. There need be no proof that the protected beneficiary was in fact a spendthrift or even had tendencies in that direction. It is enough if the third-party trustor-testator wanted to protect him. Proof that the beneficiary was sober and industrious will not vitiate the restrictions which have been written into the trust and permit him to encumber his beneficial interest for the best of purposes. Most courts will enforce the protection against principal as well as income.

Mr. Vought's will established a life income trust for his wife. He directed that upon her death the principal should be paid over in equal shares to their two sons. The will provided that the corpus of the trust "shall not be assignable." Nevertheless, one of the sons made assignments to his creditors of his interest as one of the vested remaindermen of the trust. When the widow died, the assignee creditors claimed that son's one-half. The New York court denied them. Testator had a right to make the trust estate inalienable (nontransferable).

Protection of a beneficiary may also be effected through other trust mechanisms, principally discretionary power in the trustees to distribute or not distribute as they see fit. Such a provision fits naturally when the trust is for the support and education of young people. If Johnny is a dropout and drifting — no distributions, or only meager bread-and-butter distributions until he straightens himself out. A trustee may impose conditions prerequisite to distributions to the wayward beneficiary if the trust instrument authorizes it to do so. The trustee may be instructed to back its drastic decision by a written recommendation from a named person — perhaps Uncle George or Aunt Olivia, if still alive and competent. Provisions authorizing the sprinkling of income can be used as a shield to protect beneficiaries against the results of their own foolish acts.

## Income and care of beneficiaries

Instructions to the trustee in respect to distributions of income and care of beneficiaries are part of the very heart of the trust. For most families, there is no great difficulty in reaching a decision:

All the income to my wife Janet and in the event of her death to our children share and share alike and to the issue of a deceased child *per stirpes.*

This is almost a pattern for well-to-do (but not truly rich) families during their middle years. And for husband and wife in more modest circumstances, as long as both live.

But with a change in the financial or personal situation, grave questions appear which testator must answer:

Will a wife or husband protest too violently if the trustee is given sprinkling powers, with the advantages already described?

If income from the trust plus all funds available to her from other sources may be inadequate to support the mother, will the children be restive if the instruction is to pay her yearly a named sum or 8 or 10 percent of the then value of the trust — regardless of income — knowing that this will diminish the corpus of the trust eventually reaching the second generation? And particularly when coupled with an authority to draw generously on principal to meet emergencies?

When there are several beneficiaries, should the trustee compartmentalize the estate, a separate trust for each, so that they will not quarrel in respect to their requests to the trustee? Illustration: One wants growth stock; another, maximum income.

At what amount in dollars does more income become a detriment to a child — at the age of eighteen? — at age twenty-one? — at age twenty-five? At what point in time should a child receive his or her full percentage share of income, regardless?

And if there is a ten- or twelve-year span between the eldest and youngest child — should the eldest and those down the ladder of years wait until the youngest reaches your appointed age for distribution of all income? Remember that the older children had the benefit of living parents longer than did the youngest. Perhaps the latter deserve additional dollar protection; certainly so if funds be limited.

When first presented, the question of distibution of income may seem easy to answer. As problems are probed and proliferated, testator may not be as certain.

Will the cash flow permit a mandatory $200 a month for ailing Aunt Alice? Once allocated to Aunt Alice, can it be reduced if the expenses of the surviving wife turn out to be greater than anticipated?

Testator may decide the sprinkling idea does not appeal; in his view, "No trust officer should so dominate our family." A man might ask himself: "Do I know that at the time of my death my estate will justify, say: 55 percent to my wife and 45 percent divided between our three children?" About $4,500 would be saved each year in taxes measured by income. But during a prolonged period of business stringency, the income from the estate might shrink an unbearable amount, and "my wife would not receive enough. Shall I cut the percentage to the children if her income needs to be increased? Or should I put a floor of $25,000 a year on distributions to my wife?" The allocations of income should be thought through by every testator, each in the family's factual setting.

Except for large estates where radical cuts in income would still leave a good margin of sufficiency and where emergencies could surely be met out of current funds, I assume liberal provisions for drafts on principal to pay for a prolonged illness or other calamity. However, as will be emphasized in Chapter 13 under the heading "Drafts on Principal" (page 398), when taxes are a significant factor, the authority to invade trust principal should conform to the requirements of the Internal Revenue Code and regulations.

## SPECIAL INSTRUCTIONS; DISTRIBUTION OF PRINCIPAL

The word "distribute" is commonly used in two frameworks of reference. The first refers to the distribution of the estate by the probate court to whoever may be entitled to it under the will or, if no will, under the laws of descent and distribution. Usually, all concerned desire that to be accomplished as expeditiously as possible. A small and simple estate clearly below the beginning of the bite of federal taxes may be wound up and distributed within a few weeks of death. With larger estates, the matters and procedures which must have attention take much longer. But with an occasional exception, the goal is to distribute the estate to those entitled to receive as soon as is feasible.

In sharp contrast to speedy distribution during postmortem proceedings, testator's second wish may be that her or his property be held by the trustee as long as the substantive law permits.

The scheduling of distributions from the principal of the trust may be one of the most elusive decisions faced by the testator-trustor. I will inventory a few typical formulas, some with comments. In all of them, testator is assumed to be father or grandfather.

### *Upon death of widow*

Testator's children were already adults when the will was signed. He would be following a familiar pattern if he were to instruct:

> Upon the death of my wife my trust estate shall be divided among our four children, name them, share and share alike, and to the issue of a deceased child *per stirpes.*

Here testator has faith that his grandchildren will make satisfactory marriages so that the surviving spouse of a deceased grandchild would prove a good guardian of the property thus routed to testator's great-grandchildren.

If not, testator can keep his property in trust for his descendants to the limit set by the rule against perpetuities. (See Glossary.)

### *Upon death of widow and arrival of youngest child at maturity*

Upon the death of my wife or our youngest living child reaching the age of————years, whichever event last occurs, my trust estate shall be divided among our four children and the issue of a deceased child *per stirpes*.

Note that in the topic heading, the word used was "maturity," not "majority," which in some states is a mere eighteen years of age. Testator may prefer twenty-five. Or one-half at twenty-five and one-half at thirty. Or one-third at twenty-five, one-half the remainder at thirty, with the balance at thirty-five. Or some other formula.

Here we squarely face major policy questions. At what age should a young person receive substantial wealth? Need, or even should, all children be treated alike as to date of distribution? With both the above programs comes an underlying query: "Do my wife and I want the share of a *deceased* child of ours to go direct to his minor children? The other parent will be the guardian. Do we want our money in the parent's hands, perhaps dominated by a new husband or wife?"

My answer to the questions will be, as nearly as I can remember, by repeating what was taught me many years ago by a wise couple. Under adverse conditions for two generations, that family had maintained wealth and an honored position in the community. Their two children, a son and daughter, had been born to them rather late in life and were both in their early teens when the new will was drawn.

I assumed no large distributions of principal from the husband's estate as long as the wife should live, then staggered distributions to the two children, retaining the share of a deceased child in the trust for grandchildren. But "No," the instruction was quite different. He told me:

Upon the death of my wife my trust shall be divided into two, a Son's Trust and a Daughter's Trust. Except as to distribution the instructions to the trustee bank shall be the same.

### Son's Trust

Upon the death of my wife or my son reaching twenty-five years of age, whichever event last occurs, one third of my Son's Trust shall be distributed to him to be his absolutely.

When he reaches thirty, one half of the remainder shall be so distributed. And when he reaches thirty-five years, he shall receive the balance.

If his mother lives beyond his thirtieth birthday, two thirds or all, as the case may be, shall be distributed to him upon her death.

## Daughter's Trust

My Daughter's Trust will not be the same. Her income from her trust will be ample. There will be no drafts on principal except, in the sole discretion of the trustee, in order to meet dire need.

Upon my daughter's death her trust shall be continued for the benefit of her children and theirs as long as the law permits.

I must have shown surprise. No question was asked, but he continued:

You wonder why I propose to treat them so differently. We believe in family harmony. I do not want my wealth to be cause for dissension. I would be glad to have my daughter marry a preacher, or a teacher or a composer, if they seemed devoted to each other, but I would not want him to have any part in my family investments.

She may marry a prosperous business

or professional man; he will not need my capital. She may marry a very poor business man who, nevertheless, is a loving husband and father. I have no objection to him, but I feel compelled to protect her against him. When he comes to her and says he must have a large sum to save his failing business or would like capital again to start a new business, I want her to reply:

'My beloved, you know I cannot draw on the trusts. Mama and Papa wrote them that way. Believe me, I would if I could but I cannot. I will help you by spending no more than the trust income for our household and the children.'

Now as to my Son's Trust. He is much like his uncle. I think I understand him. If he receives the first third at age twenty-five or thereabouts he will soon lose it in improvident speculation. The one third he receives at age thirty — I hope he will not lose it; I fear he will. If he loses the final third, he is no son of mine.

Incidentally, as of today, that family has

maintained its financial stability for another quarter-century.

One evening, at another family conference before the fireplace regarding the estate plan for the oldsters (both over eighty), I heard the one daughter and her husband urge that she be bypassed completely and that her half be kept in trust for their children. The daughter's husband had become wealthy; they did not want higher income taxes.

All present agreed that her brother's half should go to him without restrictions.

And so it is that I believe that the strong presumption in favor of treating children equally does not extend to time of distribution. Every situation should be carefully weighed — magnitude of estate; health, abilities, and probably needs of beneficiaries.

## Upon death of last of a class

Not infrequently, a natural time to distribute an estate is upon the death of the longest living of a class.

Upon the death of my last surviving child my trust estate shall be distributed to my then living grandchildren, share and share alike, *per capita,* and to the issue of a deceased grandchild, if any there be, *per stirpes.*

Here the visible grandchildren, each a person to testator and his wife, will receive the same amount. But the grandchildren's children are to receive only their parents' share. Testator believed their potential arrival on the scene too remote to put them on a *per capita* basis.

### *Partial capital distributions*

All things having been considered, an instruction (not merely an authority) to make a distribution of a specified amount upon the request of a beneficiary for a particular purpose may be justified. For example: $25,000 to help buy a house.

## Upon the happening of an event

A variety of illustrations are available.

When the deacons of the Tanglewood Community Church prove to the satisfaction of the trustee of my trust that the Church has in hand no less than $1,000,000 in funds and viable pledges for the construction of a new church edifice, it will distribute $100,000 to the building fund and when the architect certifies that the new structure is three-fourths completed, the trustee will give the church another $100,000 to be expended for the acquisition of a pipe organ in memory of my mother.

## Exhaustion of trust

Over the years, drafts on trust principal to meet the express purposes of the trust may have been such that the corpus is reduced to a point where a trust is no longer justified. Or through natural calamities or bad management the trust estate has become minuscule. Some testators prudently (pessimistically?) prepare for that eventuality by providing something in the nature of this statement.

If the assets of the trust should be reduced to a net value of less than $25,000, in sole discretion of the trustee it may be terminated. Assets shall be distributed to the competent beneficiaries then entitled to receive (or to guardians of incompetents and minors) in the proportions they are then receiving income.

## Discretionary distributions

It is possible to give the trustees authority to distribute principal to whom, when, and in such amounts as they deem best. Testator may supply formulas to guide the trustees when making this important and final decision. In effect, it is a power of appointment for the sprinkling of principal.

As to this segment of their financial lives, the trust beneficiaries are wholly in the hands of the individual trustees or a trustee bank, acting through trust officers. So when it comes to an aspect of the trust relationships such as this, there is no escape from a people problem.

Testators must ask themselves certain underlying questions: The trustees or trust officers will have a time advantage; they will see the estate and beneficiaries after my departure. But will they be able to fix a better timing than I can today as I sign my will? Will this discretionary power in the trustees tend to motivate the beneficiaries toward a higher level of performance?

If the trustees are burdened with this authority, they are entitled to protection against complainers. The decision of the trustees must be final and binding on all concerned.

This discussion of trusts as trusts may properly conclude with two very human examples of the flexibility of a simple trust concept. The estate of the aged Rev. and Mrs. Henry Carson approaches $100,000. They have two adult chldren; no grandchildren and none in prospect. Their divorced daughter, Ms. Valerie Whitcomb (aged fifty-one) owns and operatives a lucrative style shop. Her year-younger brother, Hadfield, imagines himself an artist whose paintings will one day be recognized as masterpieces. Presently he averages about $125 a painting, less commissions; buyers are infrequent. He lives in his attic studio which boasts a kitchenette and good northern light. He borrows, no return actually expected, from his sister and parents.

Although not truly a solution of Hadfield's fiscal problem because $100,000 principal less one-half to Valerie is not enough, a trust of orthodox pattern seems the best amelioration. Ms. Valerie is competent to be trustee first for her surviving parent and then for Hadfield; of course, with a bank as successor trustee. But to put her in that position might — would — lead to unbearable friction between brother and sister.

So the diagnosis follows the classic trust pattern.

1. On the first death, all in trust to a bank to provide for the survivor of the

Rev. and Mrs. Carson, supplementing their minuscule retirement allowance from the church.

2. Upon the second death, one half to Valerie and one half held in trust for Hadfield.

3. If either brother or sister should predecease a parent, on the second death all property would be held in trust for Hadfield or would vest in Valerie, as the case may be.

4. If neither should survive both parents, all to the church.

No bank would rejoice if offered this trust. But one would accept it as a service and sincere measure of goodwill to a preacher's family. Also, several influential members of the congregation might be grateful.

Possible variation: Ms. Valerie might welcome being kept under the trust, thus having a nest egg from mercantile hazards.

That was a testamentary trust. An *inter vivos* trust was a tool in solving the fiscal problems of Dr. Gloria A. Sandring.

She was a superlative pediatrician. She enjoyed a large income. Engrossed in her practice, she had no inclination to learn how to conserve her savings. She was happily married to a professor of philosophy who taught at a small church-oriented college not far from their home. His salary was minuscule when contrasted with her professional income.

He felt no envy; they were good parents to three fine children. A neighbor might opine that he was more of a mother than was the doctor. He had abundant time at home. She did not, and she employed a competent housekeeper, paying her, some said, almost as much as her husband earned.

Quite out of character, the professor deemed himself an astute investor. He honestly thought his habitual losses were due to unforeseeable economic factors beyond his control or anticipation.

Dr. Gloria finally observed that there was little growth in the net worth of the family; her surplus earnings were channeled to absorb investment disasters. What should she do? She did not want money, or the loss of it, to disrupt family harmony.

Properly philosophical, her spouse said he would go along with whatever she worked out with her attorney and a respected trust officer. They developed this program:

1. Household expenses, cost of children's education, and all family expenditures would be charged against the doctor and her husband on a realistic formula — leaving him savings from his salary to invest.

2. A contract separating their financial interests would be so worded as to preserve their right to joint income tax returns.

3. A covenant would be drawn by the professor stating that all his ventures would be denominated: "In my separate estate with no liability on the part of my wife."

4. Dr. Gloria would establish a revocable *inter vivos* trust into which, each month, she would pour her surplus funds. All investment responsibilities

were placed in the lap of the trustee bank.

From an abundance of caution, her attorney required that the professor employ independent counsel to represent him incident to documentation of their fiscal program.

The physician, the philosopher, and their progeny all lived happily ever after.

# EIGHT

# Agreements, Autonomous Assets, Life Insurance

Agreements may control, at least in part, what a will must say. The consideration for the promise of the prospective testator may be to provide kindly care during the final years, marriage during a more vigorous period, provision for children, or other lawful desiderata.

Several types of ownership are so attuned to the estate-planning process that they must have special attention when planning a will. Examples include joint savings accounts with right of survivorship vis-à-vis a bank account in testator's name alone; often, series E bonds; a life tenancy; the proceeds of employee benefit programs.

Then there is life insurance. It is of

great magnitude and generates the largest cash flow not usually subject to the terms of the will.

First, we will examine typical agreements tied to the disposition of property at time of death. Then we will look at specialized ownerships, and finally, at life insurance.

## AGREEMENTS ABOUT WILLS

A legally binding commitment in respect to specified mandatory provisions of a will can be a most useful device for the accomplishment of ends beneficial to, and desired by, both parties to the contract. But disadvantage is inherited in an enforceable contract concerning your will. Like an *irr*evocable trust, the will takes on an undesirable finality. To the extent it is covered by an enforceable contract, the will cannot be changed except by mutual consent. It is no longer ambulatory.

## To assume care of the aged or their property

The classic type of agreement to will property to a named person is, for example, the agreement between an aging farmer and his son, or grandson, or other young farmer who lacks land.

If you, Bill, and your wife Mary, will take over the farm and let me live with you in the big house during my remaining years, upon my death you shall have the farm, all livestock and equipment.

Bill and Mary neglect to put their agreement in writing. They move to the farm. For several years Bill tills the fields. Mary keeps the house, including caring for the slowly dying man, who also neglects to make a will giving effect to his promises to Bill and Mary. On his death, various heirs claim the farm. The oral contract having been clearly proved, backed by unquestioned performance by Mary and Bill, the court awards all to them.

Similar arrangements may of course be made regarding urban assets — a machine shop, a house, anything. But a contract concerning a will should be in writing, carefully drafted, and a contemporaneous will executed conforming to the contract. In another instance, the oral contract might not be provable.

## *Antenuptial agreements*

A marriage settlement is often a desirable preliminary to a second or subsequent marriage, and sometimes to a first marriage when either bride or groom already owns significant property. An antenuptial agreement does not sound very romantic in the American tradition. But, sooner or later, it may lubricate family relationships and prevent internecine warfare among claimants to a decedent's property.

Assume a marriage between a widower, aged sixty-five, and a widow, aged fifty. Both have grown children and each has considerable property. It may prevent misunderstandings if their antenuptial agreement provides that their properties will be kept separate, and upon the death of either, will revert to his or her children. The agreement should provide for a sufficient life estate for the survivor if there is any question as to the adequacy of the property of either spouse to finance their customary standard of living and meet emergencies.

Or assume that instead of marrying the wealthy widow, aged fifty, this sixty-five-year-old prosperous widower had married a young woman of thirty-four, with two children under ten years of age and no money. She would give up a good job in order to marry him. Do not she and her children deserve the protection of an agreement that the groom's will shall contain provisions assuring the education of the bride's children, as well as providing a minimum income for her?

The nature of community property is described in Chapter 12. The fact is stressed that, in a community property state, an antenuptial agreement may be important to the bride who marries a man with large holdings of separate property.

## *To accomplish an avowed objective*

A husband and wife in comfortable circumstances may not want testamentary trusts in their wills. They prefer to devise and bequeath all direct to each other, even though this route leads to higher taxes on the second death. But each has one worrisome reservation. What if the survivor should remarry and will a good portion, or even all, of their property to a new wife or husband?

The dilemma might be solved by an agreement demanding that the survivor will keep in effect a will leaving to their children not less in value than half of what he or she (the survivor) possessed after distribution under the will of the first to die. If the total at the time of the second death had shrunk to less than half, their children would receive all. Such a covenant regarding survivor's will would assure the first to die that his or her half would not go into strange channels. But, unless the *new* second spouse affirmed the arrangement in an antenuptial agreement, there might be controversy. For example, the second wife might assert dower rights or a community interest if the second marriage lasted several earning years.

The formula sketched in Chapter 4 (page 82), designed to keep Nora the nurse at her post as long as grandfather lives, is an example of a pinpointed covenant regarding the substance of a will.

### Joint and mutual wills

There are real as well as verbal differences between a joint will and mutual wills. A joint will is one where the same instrument is made the will of two or more persons and is jointly signed by them. Such wills, rare in the totality of wills, are usually executed to make testamentary disposition of jointly owned property.

When two or more persons make separate wills containing mutual or reciprocal provisions in favor of one another, the documents may be called "mutual wills." To illustrate:

The provisions would be reciprocal and complement each other if the wife's will left her interest in the farm to her husband, and if the husband should predecease her, to their son; and if the husband, in like fashion, left the farm to her and then to their son.

A joint will may include reciprocal provisions, making it a joint and mutual will.

Contrary to what most testators probably imagine, the mere execution of mutual wills does not impose a contractual obligation on either party to keep that will in effect. If there is a clear contract to do so, it is of course binding. And sometimes, in an ambiguous situation, the court will find an implied contract freezing the wills.

Not long ago, there was a case involving Citizens Southern National Bank and Leaptrot. After the death of her husband, the widow Leaptrot made a new will disposing of property in a fashion inconsistent with the mutual will she had executed at the time her husband made his. They both had been expressly executed as "mutual wills." There was joint ownership of property. The Supreme Court of Georgia found sufficient *implications* of an agreement to justify an implied contract between the spouses under which the survivor was bound to keep his or her will in effect.

Had an agreement been spelled out — one page would have been enough — there would have been no occasion for a law suit. Any commitment by prospective testators in respect to the attractive-sounding "joint and mutual wills" should be made only after disclosure of family business affairs to counsel and consideration of his recommendations. After all, in the Leaptrot case, perhaps the spouses did not truly want or expect the wills to be unchangeable.

Joint wills, mutual wills, and joint and mutual wills often result in ambiguity rather than clarity. A marital deduction (see Glossary) may be imperiled. Separate wills, supplemented by an unambiguous agreement, usually are a better way.

## AUTONOMOUS ASSETS OFTEN NOT GOVERNED BY WILL

In most estates, there are assets which speak for themselves in respect to who is destined to be their new owner. They do not pass under the will. A decedent might have half a million in life insurance and little else. The destination of the insurance money is determined by the contract between the owner of the policy and the insurance company — the proceeds may be outside the will or be payable to the estate and be administered under the will. So the title of this section and of that regarding life insurance might well be: "Autonomous Assets Which May or May Not Be Governed by Your Will."

Joint bank accounts with the right of survivorship predetermine ownership after the first death. In many jurisdictions, under an appropriately worded joint tenacy, the surviving joint tenant (or tenants) of realty or personalty succeeds to the ownership, regardless of what the will of decedent may say. Series E bonds are a frequent example of this principle.

When drafting a will, testator should have a memorandum of all assets which are autonomous (self-sufficient) for testamentary purposes. A decision must be made whether these assets should continue to be controlled by their own terms or whether they should be changed in nature and become subject to the plan of the will. If, for example, the will purports to provide for the care of certain aging beneficiaries, that laudable purpose may be thwarted if practically all the estate is in life insurance payable to other named beneficiaries, or in joint acccounts with survivorship rights in persons other than the beneficiaries under the will.

## Joint tenancies with the right of survivorship

The comments which follow do not apply to appropriate amounts in joint bank accounts with right of survivorship, series

E bonds, joint ownership of their home, and other joint ownerships which fit the family's pattern of life. A joint bank account with the right of survivorship is particularly useful. There is no interruption of the right to draw checks.

The comments are limited to situations where husband and wife or others create joint ownerships with right of survivorship in investment properties in the hope of avoiding taxes or postmortem procedures.

Subject to the vagaries of a particular jurisdiction, joint ownership may be a useful tool for financing. There may be a satisfaction in owning an asset together. But it can create knotty problems, both before and after death. Unanticipated taxable gifts may stem from putting property in joint names. Buying a home or series E bonds is free of this burden.

The ambulatory will may be revoked or amended, as testator's balance sheet and desires in respect to beneficiaries change. Once there is a joint tenancy, the tenants are subject to mutual agreement to escape. If the value of the joint tenancy is large in relation to the entire estate, it may prevent the allocations which, with the passage of time, testator wishes to make.

If comprehensively drawn, the wills of the joint tenants will not ignore the jointly owned property. Why, if it goes to the other? Kismet has not informed the two (or occasionally more) joint tenants which one will die first, how long a survivor will live, or whether both, or all, will go in a mass accident. Unless the disposition of the property on the second death is covered by a will, an orderly job has not been done by the planners and draftsmen.

It is rare indeed that *all* one's property can sensibly be put into joint tenancy with a right of survivorship. If done with a minimal estate below the thrust of taxes, no harm should ensue. If done with an estate within the impact of federal and state taxes, postmortem management burdens will not be lessened; indeed, the untangling of artificial ownerships might waste time.

The prestigious Research Institute of

America makes studies of legal, tax, and accounting problems. Recently it issued a special report entitled: *Should You Own Property Jointly?* Recognizing that there are drawbacks to joint ownership, the report considers the pros and cons with major emphasis on income, gift, and estate tax considerations. A sampling of subject titles indicates the scope of the inquiry: (1) "How Joint Ownership Causes Tax Difficulties," (2) "Disadvantages of Joint Ownership," (3) "Joint Ownership No Substitute for Will," (4) "Joint Bank Accounts — The Hidden Tax Pitfall," (5) "Death of Co-Owner Causes Trouble," and (6) "Complications in Owning U.S. Savings Bonds Jointly."*

Recognizing that the very term "joint ownership" has charm for many people faced with problems such as the foregoing, my caveat must be: Do *not* switch to joint ownerships as part of your estate planning except on unequivocal

*Reprinted by special permission of the Research Institute of America, Inc., New York. Copyright, 1974.

236

recommendation of counsel and assurance that in your state it is to your advantage to do so.

An agreement between husband and wife, often called a Community Property Agreement, is available where the community property law permits. It passes decedent's half of the community property direct to the surviving spouse, outside the will. Many lawyers favor its use in uncomplicated situations, with limited assets, all of which are destined to go to the surviving spouse. Pointing, by way of illustration, to the possibility of death in a common accident or an inheritance received by either husband or wife so that no longer is everything community property, other lawyers believe that simple wills are better. If you live in a community property state (see Glossary), your lawyer will have a viewpoint applicable to your family's affairs.

## Life estates

A life estate is an ownership limited to the life of the owner or (rarely) of some other person. The county buys Quinby's 620-acre farm for a park. Mr. and Mrs. Quinby reserve a life estate in the house and surrounding 5 acres. Upon their deaths, the 5 acres and the buildings pass to the county, regardless of what the Quinby wills may say. Thus the end-result is as though the parcel had been held in trust for the county.

If a succession of individuals were involved, things might not be as simple as this illustration sounds. What if the owner of the life estate failed to pay property taxes? Or defaulted on the fire insurance premium and the remainderman (the person who follows the life tenant) had not taken out coverage to protect his or her eventual interest in the building? The nub is: You must not assume that these special arrangements work automatically in your favor. Put the burden on your lawyer to protect you.

One more illustration: A father and

mother may make mutual wills devising a life estate in the farm to their childless son Arthur. They direct that upon Arthur's death, the farm be sold and the proceeds divided among their grandchildren (Arthur's nephew and nieces) or the issue of a deceased grandchild. Arthur's will cannot affect the farm. His ownership is for life only. Here again, not all is automatic. If, Arthur gone, the grandchildren cannot sensibly agree on the procedures of a sale, a court proceeding would be necessary.

A familiar type of for-life-only ownership is that of a beneficiary under a trust. Unless the beneficiary has a power of appointment (Chapter 5, page 113), the terms of the trust, not the will of the beneficiary, determine the future of the beneficial interest in the trust.

## Proceeds of employee benefit programs

The varieties of, and variations among, programs to protect employees and their families are too numerous to permit examination here. Indeed, there would not be much point in doing so; testator cannot control them. All that is truly pertinent is that

1. The protected employee may designate a person or trust as beneficiary in the event of his death, thus keeping that asset outside his estate. It is important that he do so; he may avoid taxes on this asset.

2. The employee-testator should do so on the forms supplied by the company or those who operate the fund.

3. He should remember to execute a new form whenever he desires a change in beneficiary or a change is forced by death or other circumstance, such as divorce.

And, when making allocations under his or her will, testator must remember that these benefits pass outside the will, unless (through failure on testator's part to have a proper designation of beneficiary) the funds are paid into the estate.

A retired or senior executive may leave benefits under a deferred compensation plan. The same comments apply.

### Keogh Act funds

In 1962 the Congress passed the Self-Employed Individuals Tax Retirement Act. Its trade name is the "Keogh Act." It allows self-employed persons to establish retirement funds for themselves, thus roughly putting them on a par with corporate employees who enjoy similar benefits. A Keogh program may be a profitable income tax shelter for prosperous professional persons and may become an important asset of the estate.

The complex statutory provisions pertaining to a Keogh Trust, still in a period of legislative flux, are not proper fields for survey here. Enough to say that if you are one of the comparatively rare individuals who have interests under a Keogh Trust, your attorney may have special suggestions as you plan your will.

# LIFE INSURANCE

Life insurance may be a vital segment of an overall estate plan. Without adequate coverage, it may be impossible to write the wisest will because a keystone block is missing. To better understand the proper place of life insurance as successive wills are drawn, let us step aside for the moment and scan it.

## *Orientation as to nature*

The writing of life insurance is a phase of the most massive gambling enterprise in the world. For, stripped to its essence, insurance is naught but a bet. The girl at the airport will give you 50,000 to 1 odds that the airplane will deliver you safely to Pittsburgh.

You pay $67.50 to Old Line Gambler's Life and it will hazard $50,000 that you will live a year. That is life insurance. Reversing the coin, the company calls it an annuity. In return for an agreed payment, Gambler's Life will pay you a certain sum each month until you die. In the first instance, hoping otherwise, you are betting you will die within the year. Under the annuity, you are betting you will receive more back in monthly payments than you paid to the company.

Probably unaware of the beginnings of organized life insurance found in the records of the "Roman collegia" (artisans' associations) and of medieval guilds, in 1583 William Gybbons was insured under the pioneer English policy. It describes him as a citizen and salter of London. The premium was £8 sterling per £100 and the term twelve months. Rather expensive insurance. The insurers were merchants, banded together in a joint venture to insure Gybbons.

The idea caught on. Soon Parliament, jealous of the lives of its citizens, enacted a law to the effect that the beneficiary under a life insurance policy must have an insurable interest in the life of the insured and, if the insured did not himself arrange for the coverage, his consent. It had been discovered that deplorably often the insured came to an untimely death when there was a beneficiary with no great motivation (no family or business ties) to keep the insured alive.

The ingenious vendors of life insurance developed a host of ancillary aspects and fringe benefits, the costs of which must be added to the basic bet, the premium. As part of a package deal, some of them (double indemnity in the event of accidental death, for example) are bargains and should be attached to your ordinary life policy.

I have tried to picture life insurance in the raw because I think of it as *insurance,* not as a medium for savings replacing a balanced investment program designed to offset the shrinking dollar.

If pressed, most C.L.U.'s (Chartered Life Underwriters) will, I believe, agree that usually the right policy is an ordinary life policy which, over the long pull, will work out cheaper than term insurance. Ordinary life is not as complete an answer to inflation as is short-term insurance. Under a short-term policy, if the insured wins his bet and his wife is paid $10,000, she is paid in dollars of about the same value as were the premium dollars. But short-term policies do not always insure the long-term insurability of the insured. So ordinary life is usually better. Indeed, two decades before most people recognized the glow from the fires of inflation burning over the horizon, I heard a veteran C.L.U. tell a considerable audience that, except in rarest circumstances, he believed it morally wrong to sell other than term or ordinary life policies. It was manifest that not all his hearers agreed with him — they still had faith in the long-range soundness of the dollar and consequently in a life insurance bet enlarged into a savings account by variations, such as twenty annual payments only or endowment at a stated age, often sixty or sixty-five.

## Ownership and taxation

There is, I suspect, an impression among the uninitiated that the proceeds of life insurance policies are taxed less than they are. The federal code and IRS regulations include in a decedent's estate all those proceeds of life insurance which are (1) payable to the estate; or (2) payable to any other beneficiary under a policy of insurance in which at the time of death the insured decedent possesses any "incident of ownership," exercisable alone or in conjunction with any other person.

When the deceased — the insured, the testator — possesses no incidents of ownership at the time of death, the proceeds of the policy do not become a part of the taxable estate. Under the 1976 Reform Act gifts of life insurance policies within three years of death will not be recognized. Earlier gifts must be handled with care.

The term "incidents of ownership" is not limited in its meaning to ownership in a technical legal sense. It has reference to rights of the insured or insured's estate to the economic benefits of the policy. These include the power to change beneficiaries, to surrender or cancel the policy, to assign the policy or to revoke an assignment, to pledge the policy for a loan, or otherwise to benefit from an incident of ownership. So when, as a part of estate planning, an insured person wishes to withdraw life insurance from taxation in the estate, insured must really part with it, whether by sale or gift.

It may be said that since, 1954, *mere payment* of premiums by the insured is not an incident of ownership which brings the proceeds of the policy within his estate. However, questions may arise which, I believe, compel the conclusion that a conservative program for divesting an insured of all incidents of ownership should include plans for the payment of premiums by someone other than the insured, that is, by the beneficiaries or by a third party (Aunt Rose) as a gift to them or in connection with a business arrangement.

The tax litigation of First National Bank of Oregon in the Slade estate furnishes an illustration. An insurance agent urged Fred M. Slade to buy more insurance. It would, he said, guarantee Mrs. Slade an income independent of his estate and other insurance. The agent asserted that the purchase could be arranged so that the proceeds would be exempt from estate taxes. The scheme was this:

Mrs. Slade would sign the applications for two policies on the life of her husband. Purchased from two companies, they both were issued to her as owner and beneficiary. Mr. Slade paid the premiums. Within three years he was killed in an automobile accident. The U.S. Court of Appeals in San Francisco upheld the district court in Portland in maintaining that the "purchase of two policies in his wife's name cannot be distinguished from the procurement of the policies in his own name and immediately transferring all rights of ownership to his wife." The executor bank having failed to produce evidence overcoming the three-year presumption that the transfer was made in contemplation of death, the proceeds of the policies were taxed to the estate.

Taxation of life insurance under state laws varies greatly. Almost half the states tax all life insurance. In seventeen or eighteen states, proceeds payable to a named beneficiary (in contrast to the estate or its administrator) are not taxed. In nine states, an exemption is allowed if the life insurance be payable to persons rather than to the estate. Any excess is taxed. As of the moment, the lowest exemption is $20,000 (in North Carolina) and the highest is $75,000 (in Pennsylvania).

State statutes are in an era of change; you must inquire of your attorney. Here it is enough to remember:

1. There may be a tax saving if insurance be made payable to named individuals.

2. In your beneficiaries include cousins, nephews, nieces, uncles, aunts, more distant relatives, or friends, they may be in a relatively high state tax bracket; possibly a $1,250 tax on a $5,000 legacy. Routing your largess through exempt life insurance may save that tax. For brothers and sisters, though worthwhile, the tax saving would be less.

Caveat: Do not forget that if specific allocations outside your immediate family aggregate a significant proportion of the total estate, within the will a percentage maximum should be used to protect primary beneficiaries in the event the estate should prove to be radically less than forecast.

We leave the variant state provisions and return to overall planning:

The decision having been made that life insurance is indicated and that it should be for a certain amount, in a substantial estate three key questions are: (1) Who shall pay the premiums? (2) Who shall own the policy? And (3) to whom shall it be payable? Most testators either do not reach, or have no trouble with, those questions. They answer:

Upon my death the policy shall be payable to my wife or, as second beneficiaries, to our children. I will pay the premiums, there is no other source of funds.

But for some families there are options. To illustrate:

1. A wife earns or has inherited money. If she pays the premiums on her husband's insurance from her separate funds and owns the policy, the amount payable on his death will not be part of his estate. It will come to her without dilution by deduction of death dues. But what if she dies first? The cash value of the ownership of a policy on the husband's life may be an asset of considerable value. Her will should anticipate that contingency.

2. A close corporation or partnership considers testator as a key man. With his permission, it carries insurance on his life. It does not deduct the premiums as a cost of doing business. Upon the death of the insured, it too receives the face of the policy tax-free. The funds may be used to buy part or all of decedent's interest in the business. This supplies the executrix with tax-free funds with which to pay death dues. The redemption of decedent's stock is a

highly technical maneuver which must follow exactly the course prescribed by the law and IRS. A possible penalty for failure to play this tax game according to its rules is to have the amount paid for decedent's stock taxed to the estate as dividend income.

3. *Inter vivos* trusts are available to the affluent. Here we are talking of a trust which owns the policy and pays the premiums during the life of insured in contrast to a trust which is but beneficiary. Most life insurance trusts are funded at the inception; others by periodic gifts, which may call for gift taxes. Such gifts may be of "future interests" (meaning a potential ownership which cannot be enjoyed until some future time) and donor does not benefit from the $3,000 annual exclusion.

4. When the insured or his or her spouse funds (provides dollars for) an irrevocable trust which uses income to pay premiums on policies on his or her life, that trust income will be taxed to

the insured. So, from the income tax approach, it is better if their children finance the trust which is to pay life insurance premiums.

You will not be venturing into the area of *inter vivos* life insurance trusts without the guidance of experts. Nor, without a plan and annual gift procedures will you establish a pattern of gifts from the spouse *with* money to the one *without* substantial funds, to the end that the latter may buy and own insurance on the life of the monied spouse. If the tight rope be walked with care, an existing policy may be given by its owner, usually the insured, to someone who will herceforth own it.

Quick in its results was the gift by tax expert Berman of his air flight insurance. He bought a policy at the counter at the airport. He inscribed an assignment across the face of the policy, transferring absolute ownership to his son. A few moments later the plane crashed.

IRS asserted that the father's gift to his

son was in contemplation of death. A United States District Court overruled IRS, holding that the proceeds of the policy were not part of the estate. IRS appealed. The appellate court reversed the trial court and included the $30,000 policy in Mr. Berman's estate. The executors had failed to prove that decedent's "dominant motive" in giving the policy to his son was the accomplishment of "some specific lifetime purpose" — whatever that may mean.

Applications for flight insurance now often include spaces which make an assignment easy. But the efficacy will be uncertain until the Supreme Court of the United States speaks on this subject.

## Place in estate planning

The uses of life insurance are many. It creates an immediate estate otherwise denied most young couples. It provides protection for special projects such as the financing of a home. It may be used to assure the education of the children. It may be designed to provide a fund from which to pay death dues or to buy out decedent's interest in a business venture, perhaps both. It may be used to provide a wife with resources of her own outside the trust.

Taking out insurance should not be postponed indefinitely. The applicant has no assurance that he or she will be insurable next year. On the other hand, when written in large amounts in advance of need for more insurance, it is an expensive way of guaranteeing insurability. Of course, if the insured wins his or her bet by dying soon, the premiums paid bring a big return. But year after year those who do not die pay premiums in better dollars than the beneficiary will receive in return. Today, many beneficiaries are being paid in dollars worth less than half the premium dolars.

In recognition of this problem, riders have been developed which assure insurability. They do not themselves provide insurance coverage. They promise that the insured, during a named period, will have the right to buy ordinary life insurance within specified dollar limits without a physical examination. These desirable riders go by various names, such as guaranteed renewability, convertible life, and extraordinary life.

## Various ways of handling a life insurance trust

The decision regarding to whom and how the life insurance is payable may be as important as the determination of how much should be carried. The preponderance of a family's insurance is apt to be on the life of the principal earner. Assume a prosperous but not wealthy business executive or professional man. He is insured in the amount of $75,000. Except for the family home and usables, his estate will be in two trusts — one-half in the marital deduction trust and one-half in a residuary trust.

In his jurisdiction, there is a saving in state taxes if his life insurance is payable to the wife or children. The estate will be in need of funds with which to pay death dues. The wife would like a tidy sum not subject to the trust. The testator-insured makes his policies payable $25,000 lump sum to wife and $50,000 to the estate, electing to pay a few dollars more in inheritance taxes in order to give greater liquidity to the estate.

Or suppose the insured has little more than his insurance of the face value of $100,000. He is sixty-five and his wife is sixty. Neither wants a trust. Nor would he want his widow, growing older each day, to have investment and spending control over $100,000. He wills his modest estate direct to his wife and elects to have the insurance payable to her in monthly installments for life. The monthly payments to her will be calculated in relation to her life expectancy at the time of his death. He can increase the amounts by decreasing the "years certain" during which the installments are to be paid from the conventional twenty to ten or even by foregoing any guaranty by the insurance company as to number of years. With no stipulated number of years certain, if the wife is seventy-five when he dies, she will receive $11,100 a year for life. If ten years certain be guaranteed, her annual payments will be $9,863 for life; if twenty years certain, her annual payments will be $7,870. The returns vary somewhat among companies.

A few moments ago, we were considering a relatively rare phenomenon, a somehow-funded trust which owns and pays the premiums on a life insurance policy. More frequently, life insurance trusts are established by the insured (more precisely, by whoever designates the beneficiary) at banks to receive, administer, and distribute the insurance funds in accordance with the terms of the trust. Trust officers are correct when they assert that when the proceeds of an insurance policy are turned over to the bank as trustee, there can be greater flexibility in administration and distribution. The wishes of the insured (the testator) can be followed, as under a testamentary trust. An insurance company — its head office perhaps 3,000 miles away — is bound by rigid elections as to how payments shall be made.

There are contra arguments. If the proceeds are left with the insurance company, there is the widest spread of investment risk; the occasional very bad investment by the insurance company is not from your funds. In contrast, a bank's investment department may make a disastrous decision chargeable wholly against your trust estate.

And the apparent cost: The bank's charge will be in the order of three-quarters of one percent of the entire estate per annum. The operational charge of the insurance company against the funds being held for you is not so visible.

Sometimes testators fear that if they make their life insurance payable to a life insurance trust, the estate may not have sufficient liquidity to pay debts, taxes, and administration expenses. This need not be a problem. The trustee may be given the power to purchase assets from the estate or to make loans to the estate in order to provide it with the necessary liquidity.

If you do decide to have a life insurance trust, it should be tailored to the needs of your family. When timely, in course of postmortem proceedings, the insurance funds may be poured into testator's residuary trust so that there is but one trust, perhaps reducing trust fees. Or, if counsel so advises, the assets of the estate may be channeled into an already-established insurance trust which contains instructions from the insured (the testator, now the decedent) that are the equivalent of those found in a testamentary trust. There need not be two distinct and separate trusts (at different banks, perhaps) unless you want them. If the testator wishes to use a bank but is reluctant to have investment risk concentrated in the family's trust, he or she can authorize or direct the bank to utilize one of its common trust funds. Therein, the assets of many trusts are mingled and risk of loss is diluted.

Policies contain optional modes of settlement in addition to those already mentioned. There are fixed period-payment options, fixed amount options and life income options. Sometimes the proceeds are left with the company at interest, with options available to the beneficiary. Unless the policy owner has predetermined method of payment, beneficiary may elect. This is an ancillary aspect of postmortem flexibility.

The determination of how much life insurance, to whom, and how payable may be a paramount phase of the planning of the estate. Insurance upon the life of her husband, large in amount for people of their financial status, solved the situation faced by Amy Berwick. She was a vice-president of a well-favored corporation. In thirteen years, at age sixty-two, she would be retired with a comfortable pension. Her husband, also forty-nine years of age, was a skilled blue-collar worker; but his assignments were seasonal. He lacked business acumen. Year after year, her take-home pay exceeded his. And she had received an inheritance of about $90,000. It was prudently invested.

Their problem was their daughter, Christine, who was retarded. The prognosis for a good job or satisfactory marriage was not bright. After the death of the parents, Christine would need more subsidy than the income from a $90,000 nest egg would provide.

Fortunately the husband enjoyed good health. Amy arranged for insurance upon his life with a face amount of $100,000 and the one fringe feature of double indemnity in the event of accidental death. She paid the premiums from her separate funds and owned the policy. He was merely the insured — the subject of the bet between her and the insurance company. Should Christine predecease her, Amy could cancel or continue the policy in full or as prepaid insurance in a lesser amount.

The proceeds of the policy were payable to a trustee bank. She concurrently put her $90,000 in trust with that bank with instructions to use income for the payment of life insurance premiums and accumulate the excess, subject to her instructions.

She thought that, barring an accident, she would outlive her husband. If she did not, the premiums upon the life insurance would still be paid. The father was devoted to his handicapped daughter and Amy had full confidence that he would continue to do his very best for her if he should be the surviving parent.

Upon the death of both of them, their daughter would have the security of a trust amounting to more than $200,000, including Amy's separate property and all the parents' savings; $300,000 if the father's death was accidental. The life insurance policy lifted their estate from a marginal amount in relation to its objectives to an adequate total.

## NINE

# Postmortem Management

It is impossible for an owner of considerable property to plan wisely regarding the management and disposition of assets after the accustomed guidance is no longer available without knowing what departure by death may suddenly entail. The mission of this chapter is to tell the nature of the procedures which follow the death of a person whose estate is large enough to be taxed by the federal government. It might be entitled "Duties of, and Hurdles Facing, Your Executor."

Chapter 11 is concerned with advance preparation for this interregnum period which follows the death to the end that inescapable procedures be as provident as possible. In between, Chapter 10 considers small, simple estates.

## WILL CONTESTS

Exposure to a will contest cannot be ignored. But if the will is carefully drafted and executed, the threat is usually no more than an idle specter. In Chapter 1 (page 11) it was shown that the mental qualifications prerequisite to will making are not high. The corollary is that it is usually impossible for a contestant to set aside a meticulously drawn and properly executed will.

Of course, there may be challenges beyond the control of testator; forgery is one. I suppose that if the proffered will were forged, the alleged testator would want contestant to win. Or someone may assert that the signing was procured by fraud or undue influence. Here again, if testator could return and be in court, he or she would personally oppose the admission of a deceitful will to probate.

Or it may be alleged that, though valid when made, the will had been revoked.

The discussion of intentional revocations appears in Chapter 2 (page 42). With the original signed will on the bench of the judge, unless contestant has a document reciting revocation, it is very difficult to prove that the will which was once valid has been revoked.

So we come to the haunting point — did testator have the mental capacity to know what he or she was doing? If there is *any* doubt as to mental capacity, witnesses to the signing should be carefully chosen with that in mind.

Cautious testators who believe there will be a problem may wish to make a token bequest ''and no more'' to contestants, if any should appear. The subject is discussed toward the end of Chapter 4 under ''No-Contest Provisions'' (page 108).

## THE COURTS AND BUREAUCRACIES

Your estate is subject to the laws of two governments, federal and state. Between them they:

1. Enforce the directions of the testator in respect to the disposition of his estate

2. Protect the rights of creditors

3. Safeguard the interests of minors and incompetents

4. Collect taxes incident to the passing of property at death

It is obvious that the handling of the estate of a decedent cannot be left laissez faire within each family. There may be devious and grasping, as well as honest and loving, survivors. Through its courts and bureaus, society must provide suitable routines for the attainment of the four ends just listed.

Governmental agencies and bureaucrats to be satisfied by the postmortem managers of a substantial estate include:

1. The probate court in, it is hoped, but one state, though occasionally in more

2. The Internal Revenue Service, certainly the Estate Tax Division and

often also federal income tax personnel

3. The tax collectors (inheritance or estate, and perhaps income) of the state wherein decedent resided

4. Plus, unfortunately, those of another state or states, if officials claim decedent also had residence within their jurisdiction

5. Bureaus, if any, with supervisory powers over a continuing business owned or operated by decedent

As you know: Upon death, preservation and management of business and property and the fulfillment of the instructions of the will or the laws of intestacy are the responsibility of the personal representatives of decedent. If the personal representative was named by will, this individual is called an executor or executrix. If there is no will, the person is called administrator or administratrix. All are personal representatives.

Their duties divide naturally into two divisions: (1) the lesser, the in-court probate proceedings; and (2) by far the major, the actual postmortem management of decedent's affairs and distribution of his or her property. A foretaste is found in the listing of governmental agencies and functionaries just given.

We will (1) examine in-court probate proceedings in proper perspective, then (2) survey typical tasks of the overall postmortem management during the transition period between death and the legally effective transfer of decedent's property to those who should have it, free of taxes and subject only to valid liens (for example, a mortgage) if any there be.

## CONVENTIONAL COURT PROCEEDINGS

The in-court probate ritual involves but a minor, often relatively trivial, expenditure of time. Yet, as will be seen, it may prove vital to the integrity of the estate. The word "probate" stems from the Latin *probatum,* past participle of the verb "to prove." Properly used, the term "probate proceedings" includes only the procedures (petitions, notices, hearings, and orders) required by the probate law of the jurisdiction. By adoption of the Uniform Probate Code or similar enlightened legislation, many states have already made the in-court proceedings acceptably brief.

They are largely *ex parte,* which is the judicial term for proceedings responding to the application of one party only, often without the need of notice to any person. Or, if notice is required, no one is expected to, or usually does, appear in court and object to the proposed order, such as one admitting the will to probate.

Suits on creditors' rejected claims, quarrels between heirs, actions to quiet title, and other unpleasant phenomena occasionally accompany, but are not a true part of, probate proceedings as such. To put it another way: Using the term in its proper in-court meaning, probate proceedings are mostly ministerial. "Ministerial" means that which demands obedience to rules but requires no especial discretion or judgment. In efficient law offices, a skilled secretary may do most of this routine paperwork, the lawyer appearing in court *ex parte* the few times he must. Terminology differs state by state. In Wyoming a "county" and in Louisiana a "parish"; here a "probate judge," there a "chancellor" or "surrogate." But disregarding terminology and variations which are not of the essence, in most jurisdictions the in-court proceedings are basically easy. If the probate proceedings require undue time and expense, the legislature of that state has been derelict in its duty to streamline and modernize the probate code. The Uniform Probate Code has been drafted for its convenience.

The progression of an in-court probate proceeding usually is:

1. Give notice, if any is required, whether by publication in a paper, posting on a bulletin board at the county courthouse, or by mail.

2. Prove the validity of the will. Have an order entered admitting it to probate and appointing the executor, *or*

Prove that there is no will. The court

will appoint an administrator or conservator or whatever he is there called.

3. File oath of personal representative. File bond if required. From clerk of the court secure a paper showing qualification of the personal representative to manage and distribute the estate.

4. Publish notice to creditors and send personal notices to heirs and persons named in the will, as may be required in testator's state.

The preparation of an adequate and accurate inventory is inescapable in an estate large enough to be subject to taxes. It is required by the authorities as the basis for appraisal of the estate. It may be a necessary incident to the passing of ownerships, both real and personal. If there is more than one beneficiary, it may be necessary to the very distribution of the estate as instructed by testator. Obviously, the sometimes easy and sometimes long and frustrating task of preparing the inventory is an essential procedure, whether or not it must be filed in the court proceeding. We return to court for two more quick steps.

5. Secure an order authorizing a family allowance, as generous as the judge will grant in view of the needs of the family and size of the estate.

6. If the estate is clearly solvent, secure an order (if available in your state) giving executor maximum authority.

In a growing number of jurisdictions, under modern codes, that is about all that is required in court of an executor properly named and authorized in decedent's will; the executor completes the assignment by filing a certificate showing what he or she has accomplished. Whether it is wise to forego the important advantages of a formal decree of distribution is another question. That comes when taxes have been paid or provided for and everything needful has been done.

7. The personal representative makes what is often called a Final Report and Petition for Distribution. It tells what he or she has done and makes an accounting.

As with the inventory, whether or not he is in court, the personal representative (say, a man), unless he is sole heir and devisee, would have the burden of preparing a report showing what he has done with decedent's property. If done in court, in those cases where there are minors or incompetents, the representatives will have the benefit of a scrutiny of his activities by a "guardian *ad litem,*" thus foreclosing later claims on their behalf. A guardian *ad litem* is a person appointed by the court to safeguard the interests of such folk in a particular proceeding.

8. Notice is given to those interested in the estate and a hearing is held at a scheduled hour. Usually it is *ex parte.* But if someone does wish to object, here is the proper forum.

9. After the activities of the personal representative are approved, a Decree of Distribution is entered, receipts from beneficiaries and others are filed, and the court proceedings are closed.

Outside of court, the bulk of the activities of postmortem management will have been going forward. They will be outlined shortly. To anticipate by one illustration: Obviously claims must be processed, and if the estate is solvent, those justly due must be paid, whether or not there is an in-court proceeding. The publication of a formal Notice to Creditors incident to the probate proceedings gives the tremendous advantage of a set day, usually from four to six months after first publication, within which time claims must be filed or they are banned. Without probate, a sword of Damocles may hang above the estate for a much longer, perhaps an uncertain, period of time. It will be an unusual major creditor who refrains from suit merely because no probate proceeding was commenced. In some jurisdictions, creditors themselves may start probate proceedings. They will do their utmost to reduce their claims to judgment and trace and capture the assets. The resulting embroilments may prove more complicated and expensive than the well-known, traditional forum of a conventional court probate.

And a proper Decree of Distribution, entered after the required notice to all concerned, blesses the whole proceeding with a seal of finality. It is a barrier to future claims.

## OVERALL POSTMORTEM MANAGEMENT

The personal aspects of decedent's passing must have instant attention and his or her property must be conserved and managed. The duties of those who are handling the affairs of the deceased differ with each situation and the needs of each family. If a husband dies leaving a going business and an inexperienced wife, the problems are far different from those that appear when the wife passes first, leaving a prosperous and capable husband. Or, what if they both go in a plane crash, leaving minor children?

Most of the remarks which follow apply to the majority of substantial estates. But other comments may apply to comparatively few. Indeed, the fiduciaries of decedent often do not participate at all in category 1, entitled "Very Personal." Decisions will be made and implemented by the family, seasoned by the known wishes of the departed.

And of course small estates may be an exception to most of this chapter. Already in many states (soon to come, I hope, in all), streamlined legal machinery makes it possible for estates of nominal value to pass, particularly to a surviving spouse, with a minimum of red tape and expenses. (As already stated, small and simple estates are discussed in Chapter 10.)

But, as a person of even moderate financial substance strives to draw the right will and program wisely for postmortem management, it should be borne in mind that *the following may be required of the personal representative,* the executor.

1. VERY PERSONAL. In Chapter 4 (page 84), comments are made regarding lodging of testator's personal instructions, if any, regarding the funeral and related matters. Often the executor *as such* has no function except to be helpful if he can. These are usually matters for next of kin. However, sometimes executor must participate in determinations regarding:

Funeral or memorial services or none at all? Any requests regarding priest, rabbi, or minister? Or music? A ritualistic service, as through a lodge? Pallbearers? Burial or cremation? Where? Biographical data for newspapers. Notification to relatives at a distance and others.

Data to be supplied officialdom. Death certificate: made out by doctor or funeral parlor? Who will file it and where? If cause of death is unnatural, advise police or sheriff and eventually coroner.

2. IMMEDIATE. Funds "today" for the family. Continue a going business, if any; the cows must be milked tonight. See to

safety and proper use of all decedent's property. Gather records and useful documents.

3. PROOF OF WILL AND COMMENCEMENT OF IN-COURT PROCEEDINGS.

4. INSURANCE. .

*Life:* Possible assistance to beneficiaries in collecting claims and advice in respect to elections under the policy. Set aside to pay claims or taxes?

*Other insurance:* See that personal representatives are included among the assureds where desirable. Possibly increase insurance.

5. PREPARATION OF INVENTORY. In some jurisdictions, a formal inventory must be filed in the court proceedings. With proper planning, the executor will be aided by an annotated inventory prepared by testator, as recommended in Chapter 11 (page 316).

6. FISCAL. Current management of business affairs; preparation of estate budget including tax requirements as soon as approximate value of estate is known; liquidation of assets to meet cash

requirements if sound judgment so indicates.

7. APPRAISAL. Some states require appraisal by an official appraiser, appointed by the court or state taxing authorities. In other states, the executor secures the opinion of specialists in the various fields, more or less acceptable to IRS. And even where there is an "official" appraiser or appraisers, it is often wise to secure a written appraisal from a recognized expert; on the value of jewelry, for example, or of a going business.

8. PRELIMINARY DISTRIBUTIONS. If authorized by will and solvency of estate is evident, make partial or possibly complete distributions of certain bequests.

9. CLAIMS AGAINST ESTATE. Allow in whole or in part, or resist, as facts warrant. Do not pay in full unless estate is surely solvent with no risk of need of marshaling assets — meaning the arrangement of claims so as to secure the proper application of the assets to the various claims.

10. OBLIGATIONS OWING ESTATE. Collect moneys owing to, and retrieve properties owned by, estate. Clear clouded titles.

11. PAYMENT OF TAXES. Prepare tax returns and supporting data and pay income taxes, federal estate, state inheritance or estate, and gift taxes. Resist exorbitant demands by taxing authorities.

12. FINAL DISTRIBUTION and CLOSING OF ESTATE. This may be exceedingly simple; all to one beneficiary, possibly the executor who was also named sole beneficiary. Or it may be a delicate and difficult segregation.

While, obviously, category 12 comes last and categories 1, 2, and 3 come first, the others overlap and intermingle. Results obtained in respect to claims and obligations will affect the ultimate total of the appraisal and the computation of death dues. Or, there may be no claims at all against the estate except current household bills and medical and hospital charges incident to the passing of decedent.

The foregoing checklist, broadly indicating the type of activities which face the personal representative, may suggest substantive provisions for the will. For one example: a specific instruction concerning the timing of named distributions.

Implicit throughout is the fundamental that the personal representative must keep meticulous records and document all transactions. Unless the executor is unusually capable in the keeping of accounts or has a truly expert bookkeeper familiar with testator's affairs, the books of the estate should be opened by a competent accountant who will prepare or audit the final fiscal reports. It should save costs to have such an expert in on the ground floor.

## UNDUE DELAYS

When there is delay in closing an estate, almost always it comes from something outside the legal mandates of a probate proceeding. (I must recognize, but here logically bypass, leisurely personal representatives and their dilatory attorneys: they may cause cockpit error, not attributable to equipment.) Three examples of delays which the executor and counsel could not prevent should suffice. A score could be listed, scarcely pausing to think.

1. The principal asset was timberland or a business difficult to appraise. Internal Revenue took two or three years to make up its collective mind. Tax litigation followed. It was five or six years before the estate could be closed.

2. Unexpectedly, enormous claims were filed. Without the knowledge of his wife, decedent had been speculating through the medium of a joint adventure with friends. He guaranteed the borrowing of the venture. The wife and executor resisted payment. They fought the claims to the Supreme Court of their state. The final decision in their favor was rendered close to the fourth

anniversary of the husband's death . . . well after her remarriage.

3. Testator made a mistake. He failed to mention in his will a son by an early, short-lived marriage. Adopted by the mother's second husband, the boy had been reared in the new household with half-brothers and -sisters. Direct communication with the natural father had been nil. Hearing of the death, the son, now in his fifties, contested the will. He was entitled to, and did, participate in the estate of his father in accordance with the law of the jurisdiction.

It has been recognized that very occasionally the validity of a will is challenged, either when offered for probate or later within the comparatively short period during which the efficacy of the order admitting it to probate may be questioned. A full-dress trial follows. If the court of that county are congested, there may be disgraceful delays. But probate procedures *as such* do not cause the procrastinations. It is the fault of the judicial system as a whole; its impact will also be seen on litigation not related to probate.

And, clearly, if anyone formally asserts legal rights which are not recognized in a will, claimant should have a day in court just as does every other citizen who believes there is a good cause of action against someone. If probate proceedings have been bypassed — that is, if no executor or administrator has been appointed — the lawsuit would have been brought anyway. The widow, children, remote heirs, perhaps a trustee bank, and other interested parties could find themselves directly in court. Defense lawyers might proliferate and the court proceedings become far more complicated and expensive than if an executor nominated by testator had been appointed by the judge.

## TRAUMA

What careful data would show, I do not know. But seemingly in a preponderance of probates, it is a new and traumatic experience for the principal survivor. For a surviving wife or mother, for example, it may be her first close contact with business affairs. Mysterious papers are put before her to sign. Baffling questions regarding property and business problems are asked of her. The lawyer tries to explain; he may be a good tutor. For the moment she understands. But by the next morning she is again confused and possibly almost all that was said the afternoon before has passed from her mind. That bothers her — exceedingly. She may begin to fear inadequacy for her tasks ahead as executrix, when as a matter of fact her problem is inexperience, mingled with sorrow and shock. She does not realize that it is perfectly normal for her to forget.

During their first conference, the lawyer should explain that new problems will be before her and that she cannot be expected to absorb and remember all of them; that he will be glad to retrace today's conference as often as she wants. Indeed, in many cases, a most important function of the attorney is to keep the bereaved busy with things to do. A pitcher has been emptied. It must be filled. If the lawyer devotes (and charges for!) hours showing the desolate how to do some of the many chores to be done, he may be a better servant of the estate and friend of the family than if he and his clerks do the work themselves and save quite a bit of time.

Of course, if the wife has participated in preparation for postmortem management, as sketched in Chapter 11, her path will be much easier. She will start with a basic understanding of what it is all about. In the absence of indoctrination in estate affairs prior to death, she must not be surprised or discouraged if it takes her a full year to regain her poise.

# TEN

# Small, Simple Estates

After reading the preceding chapter pertaining to management of an estate when the owner is gone and, perhaps, glancing at the next chapter (11) which suggests ways to ameliorate the problems of postmortem management, those who deem their estates to be both small and simple may well ask: "What have these two chapters to do with me?" The answer is:

If time proves you are correct in your assumption that your estate will be *both* small and simple, the descriptions of Chapter 9 and the recommendations of Chapter 11 have little application to you. However, upon reflection, you may conclude that considerable planning and self-discipline are necessary if a family with a projected "small" estate is to keep postmortem expenses to the very minimum.

The term "small" has varied meanings. An estate should be defined as seen in the eyes of the beholder. Tax people think in terms of federal taxes. The taxable estate of a married couple formerly came within the federal orbit when their estate reached $120,000 or that of a single person when it topped $60,000. Under the new law a federal estate tax return is not required unless decedent's gross estate reaches: if dying during 1977, an aggregate of $120,000; if during 1978, $134,000; if during 1979, $147,000; if during 1980, $161,000; and, ending the climb, $175,000 if the death occurs in 1981 or thereafter.

For IRS, all below those limits are, or will be, too small to tax. However, if the total of all estate assets were greater than the amounts named and were brought below the demarcation line only because of deductions and allowances of claims, the estate would end as a small, nontaxable estate from the viewpoint of the "Federals" but would not have started out that way.

I cannot agree with the lofty stance that an estate not subject to federal taxes is a small estate. My father was a preacher; only very rich families had as much as $100,000. Shrunken as is today's dollar, only very few estates will reach the federal brackets just listed.

Minimum estates which do not even reach the lower boundary of *state* taxation (usually $20,000 or less) are certainly not large. But we must remember that a $9,000 legacy may seem a fortune to an orphaned college sophomore whose target is a Ph.D., or to a widow who longs for a few spendable dollars beyond her social security checks.

As remarked in the Preface, whatever a family possesses is its financial universe. I do not consider any estate "small" in the sense of being unimportant. The $9,000 estates of the preceding paragraph were large enough to meet significant human needs. The same could be said of the smallest estate.

There is, I must admit, a point of penury

too low to touch upon. Every night, derelicts die in the flophouses with a battered suitcase and a few dollars, or none at all. Life has dealt so harshly with them that for practical purposes they leave no estate. We must begin a few strata above them.

One category cannot cover the entire range from almost nothing to the present (for five years) ascending effective exemption accorded each estate. As will be seen, instead of the traditional method of deducting an exemption before calculating the tax, one now must calculate the tax and then claim a credit on that tax.

## SIMPLE VERSUS COMPLEX

But first we must examine a cross-classification. It is between *simple* and *complex*. If the estate is both small and simple, the transfer of ownership should be swift and frugal.

Please consider these two $20,000 estates.

1. This *small and simple* estate
   consists of:

| | |
|---|---:|
| Life insurance, payable to spouse | $ 5,000 |
| Savings accounts with rights of survivorship | 10,000 |
| Series E bonds, payable also to surviving beneficiary | 5,000 |
| TOTAL | $20,000 |

2. This *small but complex* estate consists of:

| | |
|---|---:|
| A house, salable at about $17,500, subject to a first mortgage of $10,000 and a second mortgage of $5,000; net after cost of sale perhaps | $ 1,250 |
| Various odd-lot securities, some in name of husband, some in name of wife | 5,000 |
| Supposed equity in automobile | 750 |
| Life insurance, forgetfully payable to divorced wife, though not so required in the decree of divorce | 1,000 |
| Checking account, husband's name only | 250 |
| Survivorship savings accounts | 6,450 |

| Series E bonds, payable to survivor | 1,500 |
| Series E bonds, payable to one person only | 800 |
| Note evidencing loan to brother. He is believed to be solvent, but for years has procrastinated in respect to payment | 3,000 |
| TOTAL | $20,000 |

In both instances the nominal value of household furnishings and furniture and personal effects has been disregarded.

Postmortem proceedings in the first, a small *and* simple estate, need be no more than for the survivor to:

1. Pay current household bills and debts owing.

2. Pay expenses of last illness, funeral, and interment. (Utilization of lodge, union, or veterans' benefits, if any.)

3. Go to the bank and arrange for new series E bonds to be issued to beneficiary and successors.

4. Change bank accounts to survivor and successors.

5. If within the impact of state taxes, prepare and file the required form and, depending on the state, pay a nominal tax or none.

The survivor who is mobile and alert, with a modicum of business know-how, may not feel the need of even consulting a lawyer. However, such a person would be wiser to verify his or her path by at least one consultation with an attorney, to secure from him a checklist of things to do, places to go, and persons to whom to write, and to have him prepare the state tax return, if needed.

We turn to the second, a *small but complex,* estate, as above inventoried. In addition to the two savings items and life insurance which easily pass outside the will, someone must face:

*The House:* Perhaps there will be an ownership with right of survivorship so that *title* passes. But possession of title does not pay interest on the mortgages, or repay principal, or repair the roof. The house will require dealings with two mortgagees and probably an input of capital. If a sale is indicated, title must be cleared.

*The Securities:* The transfer agents — usually New York banks — must be satisfied as to the validity of the postmortem proceedings before issuing certificates in the name of the new owner. Perversely, their requirements differ.

*The Car:* A new certificate of ownership may or may not be necessary.

*Life Insurance:* Who will persuade divorced wife to relinquish $1,000 death benefit?

*Series E Bonds:* If payable to one person only, title must be cleared. (Comments follow.)

*Checking Accounts:* If in one name only, title in new owner, under will or intestacy, must be cleared.

*Note from Brother:* Someone must persuade brother to pay.

It is, I suppose, evident that this complex though small estate may consume appreciable legal time.

We should refer to procedures pertaining to the transfer of series E bonds, listed in both the simple and complex inventories. Many people purchase E bonds during their working years. No income taxes are paid while the interest accumulates. After retirement reduces earned income and the age of sixty-five brings the advantage of double exemption from income taxes, the bonds may be cashed with little or no tax impact. So they may be an excellent and safe investment for those planning for a small estate.

If simplicity in handling after death is also in the mind of the small investor, testator will have the bonds issued in beneficiary form so that ownership will pass easily, outside of probate.

There is, I think, a general impression to the effect that all the holder of series E bonds need do is take the bonds somwhere (the post office?), smile, and say: "Uncle Sam, please take these and give me new bonds.''

It cannot be made that easy. The bonds come under the jurisdiction of the Department of the Treasury. In the field, it is the Federal Reserve Bank. The bank provides forms to assist the usually bewildered survivor who is arranging a transfer on his own, without benefit of probate proceedings. They cover various situations.

Whether the transfer of series E bonds proves an easy procedure, or is a bit frustrating, depends largely on luck. If you happen to live in a big city with a Federal Reserve Bank or branch nearby, a guard will escort you to a window where there will be an expert who will tell you what you must do and precisely how to do it, handing you the proper forms. Or if, behind the counter at your own bank, there happens to be a clerk who really knows the techniques and has a supply of forms, your way will be open. But if (and this can happen at any bank) the clerk behind the counter and the nearby assistant cashier both lack know-how, you may be shuttled from place to place before your task is done.

This is not to discourage anyone from handling the minimal or small estate personally, out of court, if he or she can. I must not, however, give the impression that the transfer of ownership of series E bonds and of bank accounts is always as automatic as a vending machine.

Let us now divide estates below the lower edge of federal taxes into three categories according to size, not for a moment forgetting that because one is exceedingly simple and the other disastrously complex, estates of approximately the same value may be different in kind when it comes to costs and delays of handling. We will examine the nature of the assets a person of limited means should own at the time of death if he or she wishes to keep postmortem proceedings to a minimum.

The theme throughout will be simplicity. Like most things, this simplicity is relative. As the estate becomes larger, there can be greater variety without undue complexity at time of death. Indeed, unless there be some diversity, an estate beyond the minimum may not be well invested. I must stress — doubly stress — that I am not playing at being investment counselor to the dynamic family which sees financial growth ahead. At the moment we are concerned only with static situations where, for example, testator is certain, or at least assumes, that his estate will be minimal or small in size and that he must save every penny he can in the transfer of his assets to his spouse, or children, or parents — or whoever his successor may be.

## MINIMAL ESTATES

Minimal estates are those clearly below the lowest bite of state taxes; no one is interested except creditors and heirs.

All the assets should be such that they pass outside the will. Nevertheless, there should be a one-page will:

I devise and bequeath all I possess to my husband David.

Should he predecease me, our only

children, our daughter, Sara Smith (Mrs. Maynard Smith), and our son, Albert Knudsen, shall take share and share alike, or all to the survivor of them.

If the properties are as recommended below, there need be no court proceedings on the first death. Nor on the second, if the surviving spouse remembers to arrange with the bank to name the second wave of successors in the bonds and savings accounts.

Consistent with the discussion of autonomous assets and life insurance which you read in Chapter 8, usually the investment assets of a minimal estate should be:

*Series E Bonds*. Payable also to a survivor beneficiary.

*Joint Survivorship Savings Accounts*. If a checking account, payable to a survivor.

*Life Insurance*. Payable to a first beneficiary backed by second beneficiaries.

Within the value limits of "minimal estates," there cannot be much real estate. If a home is still owned by testators, they should have assurance from their lawyer that by virtue of whatever legal device is most appropriate in their jurisdiction (joint tenancy with right of survivorship, community property agreement, or other legal mechanism), the real estate will pass to the survivor without in-court proceedings. If by chance there is trivial real estate other than a home, perhaps it should be sold and the proceeds put into the joint savings account.

If because of advanced age, illness, or physical immobility, the survivor cannot personally do the necessary missions, and if he or she has no relative or friend to discharge these tasks, employment of an attorney is really to obtain personal services a more fortunate person could perform independently. It is not because of legal barriers.

# HOMESTEADS AND EXEMPTIONS

The definition of "minimal estate" adopted for this discussion recognizes a possible interest of creditors.

The important question to be asked by a family facing financial disaster is: "What can the creditors do to us?" Imprisonment for debt is a thing of the past in the United States. In England, it has been outmoded since 1869. Social policy puts the integrity of the family ahead of the right of the creditor to collect the utmost farthing.

This principle is seen in several garbs. Not all an employee's wages or salary can be reached by a creditor (the process may be called "attachment" or "garnishment") even though the creditor has a valid judgment against the debtor. If the creditor seeks to seize and sell the property of the debtor, the latter has "exemptions" as defined in the statutes of the state. A family which goes through bankruptcy enjoys exemptions never, it seems to them, sufficient, but a far cry from the scenes of Charles Dickens. We now carry the principle to probates.

The word "homestead" evokes the picture of 160 acres of virgin farmland, a bride in a gingham dress, and her husband with a long rifle and coonskin cap. They will cultivate a homestead which cannot be taken from them by general creditors; nor can their oxen, plow, and other tools. As evolved to current usage, in many states the term "in lieu of homestead" refers to the property (real or personal) which creditors cannot reach in course of a probate proceeding. There are other terms, "family allowance" or "exemption," for example. Property "in lieu of homestead" will be set aside by the probate court to protect an impoverished family. Legal proceedings are kept to a minimum.

As with state limits and formulas for taxation and exemptions from attachment and garnishments, the magnitude of the "award in lieu of homestead" (by whatever name it happens to be called) differs state by state. The legislative trend is steadily upward.

But the award in lieu of homestead is no

certain relief to the troubled family, even up to its modest limit which, for momentary purposes, we assume to be $10,000. What if the family's assets are complex? Setting all the minimal estate aside, "in lieu of homestead" protects against creditors. However, it must still be untangled. Satisfactory postmortem proceedings are made difficult because of the unfortunate nature of the assets.

## SMALL ESTATES

Small estates are those which begin at the assumed $20,000 bottom marker for state taxes and continue to the $40,000 range.

In this area, the adjective "small" may be appropriate, but not "nominal" or "minimal." Again resisting the temptation to think in terms of a growing estate, how should these owners plan their affairs so as to minimize cost and delays of postmortem proceedings? Actually, their planning should be pretty much as with minimal estates except that the amounts will be larger and it is likely there will be state taxes to pay.

The survivor should have professional help in preparing the tax return. Other than that, a competent survivor can manage his or her own affairs if, and only if, he or she has seen fit to follow the precept of simplicity, seasoned with a little foresight. The comments regarding life insurance, series E bonds, and joint savings accounts found under "Minimal Estates" (page 299) apply here, extended to include the possibility of benefits under pension plans. There is more apt to be a home or even other real estate. Again an effort should be made to have the family lawyer put title in such a fashion that, in the state in question, it will pass outside the will. I assume no land in another state or land held anywhere as an investment, unless long in the family.

Perhaps, as with minimal estates, the will need be no longer than one page. But with $35,000 or $40,000 in limbo, in some situations there should be special provisions, such as to help grandchildren through school. Since the estate is probably too small for a trustee bank to handle, testator might name Aunt Bertha or Uncle Donald as trustee.

If the "small estate" reaches these altitudes, there may be stocks and bonds. Bearer bonds can be briskly passed along. Often not so with stocks and registered bonds. The possessors of this "small estate" have jumped our guidelines for owners who have given up hope for growth and whose only, or at least main, objectives are economy and expedition after death.

## AVERAGE ESTATES

"Average" estates are those which are bigger than "small," but still escape the federal estate tax. Simplicity, as long as it makes business sense, is still highly desirable. Nevertheless, the rules of Chapter 11, rather than the preceding preachments regarding "minimal" and "small" estates, apply. A family with assets ranging upward from some $40,000 may own a cabin across the state line. There may be personal business ventures and a significant investment portfolio.

Perhaps now the family assets should be

preserved for someone by a trust.

I commend the study of Chapter 11 to those who possess average estates as much as to the affluent who can count their properties in higher figures. The digits may be different, but the principles are the same.

# ELEVEN

# PREPARATION FOR POSTMORTEM MANAGEMENT

This chapter was first written for senior citizens only. I presupposed that much of the subject matter would seem too remote to the couple preparing the first, second, third, and even the fourth of the sequence of wills cataloged in Chapter 2 (pages 35-38). I imagined that about all that can be expected of a virile person below retirement age is the making of a sensible will — postponing actual preparation for the postmortem management of his or her estate until the idea of death metamorphoses from a vague realization to a reality, approaching with accelerating speed.

Thinking it through, I came to the conclusion that preparation *suitable to the nature of the estate* should not be limited to retirees. Homework begins in support of the very first will. Then it will be an easy task, probably accomplished within an hour. If the estate grows in magnitude and complexity, preparation for postmortem management increases geometrically in importance.

Consequently, this chapter is written for the youngest and healthiest reader as well as for the oldest and most frail — fully realizing that for the fortunate who envisage a half-century of years stretching safely before them, actual preparation for postmortem management will seem an unnecessary exercise. But there are elderly parents who mourn for middle-aged children who have crossed the great divide before them. And a yearly recapitulation of assets and liabilities is good for any family. It tends to bolster investment perspective.

And so it is that now I say that, within practicable bounds, every testator should so organize his or her affairs that the duties and problems faced by postmortem management will be minimized. This would save many hours of work by the executor and counsel, which should translate into dollar savings for the estate.

Preparation for postmortem management falls naturally into seven sectors: (1) consolidating holdings, (2) the homeland, (3) furnishing information, (4) anticipating appraisals, (5) liquidity, (6) fees of executor and counsel, and (7) various suggestions. Note well that the word in (7) is "suggestions," not "instructions." If testator's advice rises to the status of a directive, it must be spelled out in the will itself through instructions to the personal representatives and trustees or by way of limitations upon property — for example,

I devise my summer home Whiteacres to my daughter Betsy for life, or until she no longer wishes to use it, and then to the Farm City Community Church, to be sold when deemed advisable by the Board of Deacons. The proceeds may be used for any church purpose.

(Legal location of Whiteacres should be given.)

## ON CONSOLIDATING HOLDINGS

It is amazing how much wallpaper is found in safe-deposit boxes. Not infrequently, from one to a dozen or more stock certificates carry a tantalizing though unknown name; the business beckons to be discovered. A thorough search is the duty of the executor; he may do no less. Sometimes a nugget is found. But more often the aggregate cost of hunting exceeds the total value of the mysterious speculations.

There is also a species of gilt-edge security which seldom really belongs in the strongbox of a substantial testator thriftily planning for postmortem management. It is the minute odd lot. There may be sound reasons for holding ten shares of Union Oil to day of death, but usually not. These trivial certificates are often leftovers. Testator once had 100 shares of Union Oil; he received a 10 percent stock dividend. Later he sold his

100-share block at a pleasant profit. Thinking he might buy in when the oils were undergoing a cycle of unpopularity, he retained the ten shares; the periodic reports to shareholders would keep him informed. This was his regular practice. His box is crowded with stock certificates, a few shares each, although a full 90 percent of the value of his investment portfolio is concentrated in a dozen issues.

Variations on the theme of worthless paper and petty odd lots are endless in number. The point to be made here is easy to state. When preparing for postmortem management, unless there is a discernible reason for holding, (1) take your losses (an income tax saving) and clear your box of all worthless securities; (2) liquidate or identify all unlisted securities; (3) though each is good, sell the sundry small odd lots and buy one issue.

If sale of the sound odd lots would involve irritating capital gains, testator can (1) use them for tax-free gifts up to $3,000 (Chapter 12, page 359) to each beneficiary, or (2) use that seven-share

General Electric certificate to pay a subscription to the United Fund. At present values, this solution might actually save money.

## THE HOMELAND

Testator's residence, let us assume, is in Wisconsin. Since retirement, his traditional winter visit to southern California has lengthened until, during the last two years, it extended over six months. He bought a condominium in his own name. He found it convenient to be listed in the telephone book and have an account in the branch bank at the shopping center. Wisconsin is still home; it always has been; he never thought of it otherwise.

Some years ago, testator and his sister inherited the properties of their bachelor brother, including a farm in South Dakota. They kept the farm. There was a modest rental income; bird shooting was good in the fall; and it was rather fun just to own all those acres.

In this fashion, testator set the stage for

ancillary probate proceedings in California and South Dakota, including the making of state tax returns and the payment of taxes in those states. South Dakota should present no great problem. A competent lawyer may be found at the nearby county seat. He will act as ancillary administrator and take the legal steps necessary to passing title to an undivided half of the farm to testator's devisees. (Unless the testator's sister learns a lesson, on her death there will be a replay.) South Dakota inheritance taxes will not increase the aggregate of death dues; the farm will not be taxed also in Wisconsin. But the cost of postmortem management is increased by the total of fees paid to the South Dakota lawyer-administrator plus the value of the extra time of the Wisconsin attorneys and executor required by the ancillary administration in South Dakota. Had testator and his sister been alert postmortem planners, they would have sold the farm or given it *inter vivos* to whoever is destined to have it.

Now consider California. There must be

an ancillary probate, a California attorney probably serving also as administrator. While answering the questions on the form supplied by the State Tax Commission, he will be required to disclose testator's bank account, telephone listing, and length of annual stay in the sunshine. The California taxing authorities will assert that testator has become a resident of that state and amerce death dues against all his property except the South Dakota and Wisconsin realty. This does mean more taxes, in a substantial amount. The executor decides to resist. He gathers evidence and journeys to California to attend a hearing before reviewing officers of the tax commission. The decision is against the estate. California counsel think they have a 60-40 chance of winning if they take the matter to the Superior Court in Riverside County. They do. Win or lose, it has been an expensive procedure for the estate.

By prudent planning, testator could have (1) avoided owning any property necessarily taxed in California, or (2) so handled his affairs in California that (as in South Dakota) there was no claim against the estate except the inheritance tax resulting from the ownership of the one condominium. Moral: Do not casually establish what might be considered a new domicile.

## ON FURNISHING INFORMATION

It is the rare exception rather than the rule for the personal representative of a decedent to find an orderly record of all assets of, and potential claims against, the estate. She or he must spend expensive time in developing essential data which testator could have personally provided. A prime requisite to planning for postmortem management is what might be termed an annotated inventory.

### *Your annotated inventory*

There is no occasion here to be brittle about the precise form of an inventory or a balance sheet. Perhaps you have already prepared much of what is needed

— without explanatory notes — when submitting a periodic statement to the bank as a basis for personal loans. It will be readily adaptable to your estate-planning needs. If you have no statement forms handy, the friendly neighborhood bank will provide them.

Or perhaps you will prefer to develop a statement tailored to your own situation. Following the United States Estate Tax Return the sequence of assets would be:

Schedule A: *Real Estate*

Under the Real Estate heading, identify each parcel by commonly used address, urban or rural. Tell where deed and title insurance policy or abstract and title opinion, recent tax receipts, and other pertinent papers will be found. Any recent appraisal or form offer to buy. Identify leases.

Schedule B: *Stocks and Bonds*

List all. Tell where lodged. If in your safe-deposit box, fold them lengthwise with name showing, arranged alphabetically.

Schedule C: *Mortgages, Notes, and Cash or Equivalent*

Here list each item, tell where each document can be found. Give name of each bank, the branch, and account number. Provide similar data in respect to investments in savings and loan associations and all other funds. If some are joint accounts, say so and tell source of the funds; perhaps part is not taxable in your estate.

Schedule D: *Life and Other Insurance*

List all policies (1) upon your life and (2) in which you have an interest, though upon the life of someone else. Who are beneficiaries, primary and contingent?

Tell of public liability, accident, health, automobile, fire, and all other insurance coverage.

Tell where the policies are and give status of loans against them, if any. Name your insurance agents.

Schedule E: *Jointly Owned Property*

Describe property and ventures, if any

there be (other than realty already listed under "A" and joint accounts under "C"), owned jointly or as tenants in common.

Adequately describe property and documentation, give location of instruments. Spell out your interest.

Schedule F: *Other Miscellaneous Property*

Here be careful. "Household furniture and furnishings" and "furs and jewelry" may be sufficient. Do not unnecessarily identify an item and make it sound far more valuable than it is. On the other hand, you may have a collection — Chinese snuff boxes to stamps — which should be described. Or paintings or antique furniture which cannot in good faith be ignored.

Schedule G: *Gifts Which Must Be Reported*

If you have made gifts which must be reported on your estate or inheritance tax returns, list them. Otherwise, hours may be spent searching your records. Ask your tax adviser. Make sure you have filed required gift tax returns. IRS will be watchful for gifts in contemplation of death.

Schedule H: *Powers of Appointment*
If you have the right to designate a beneficiary under another's will, identify it. (Chapter 5, page 113.)

Schedule I: *Annuities*
If you are entitled to a sum of money for life or a designated term, refer to it and the location of the controlling document.

Your total estimated value of the assets you have inventoried under Schedules A through I is your estimated *gross* estate. The total of the allowable deductions (Schedules J through O) are subtracted to reach the *taxable* estate. They are listed in the next chapter.

Your inventory sheets should be brought up to date at least annually. With them should be lodged a statement of your principal obligations, these also supplemented to the extent you think might be helpful to the executor. An 8½ x

11 inch ring binder is a convenient appliance for the development of a considerable catalog of assets and list of liabilities. As it is brought to date year by year, some pages will be replaced or updated and others left untouched.

If either husband or wife inherited property or acquired significant property prior to marriage, it is well to keep a record of it. Routing all transactions through a separate bank account used exclusively for the separate funds is a good way. Maintaining the account in a different bank from that holding the family joint account, or at least in a different branch, helps avoid confusion. When describing separate property, include data sufficient to establish its nature, date of acquisition, value at that time, present value, and source of increase if notable.

The assemblage of data suggested on the preceding pages includes much ancillary but pertinent information not found on a year-end balance sheet done by an accountant. Annual updating should be easy. Comments regarding valuations follow shortly.

## Personal and miscellaneous information

Your executor will be required to answer many questions concerning you and your affairs. Because of differences in the nature of the tax, the questions asked in the state forms may differ from those of the United States Estate Tax Return. With an annotated inventory, the meticulous planner will attempt to provide the executor with answers to questions which, on one occasion or another, he must answer.

Here follows a consolidation of those found in the federal and typical state tax returns, plus those required by the usual in-court probate proceedings, plus those your attorney may ask of you as you are formulating your will. (Chapter 14, page 408.)

*Questions about Testator:*
Full name? If known by other names, what are they?
Date and place of birth? Citizenship?

Social security number?

Domicile? (See Glossary.) When was domicile there established?

Business or occupation? If retired, former business or occupation?

Military record?

Marital status? If married, date of marriage? Name or names before this marriage? Domicile at time of marriage?

If testator is a widow or widower, name and date of death of deceased spouse?

If legally separated or divorced, date and in what court obtained? Any obligations incident to earlier marriages?

*Questions about Spouse:*

Social security and military data as above listed for testator? Any contractual obligations concerning this marriage? If so, what? If any mental or physical problem, reserve for oral report to draftsman of will.

*Questions about Children:*

Full name, date and place of birth of each of them, whether by present or former marriage?

Children's marriages? To whom?

Note special major problems of a child, whether physical or mental.

Any adopted? Stepchildren? If so, include. If there should be an illegitimate child or grandchild, or one who may claim to be, tell your lawyer.

### Questions about Parents:

If living and to be included in your will, note ages, health, and approximate financial condition.

### Questions about Siblings:

If brothers or sisters are to be named in will, name each. If any are to be left out, with others in, name them also and briefly indicate why.

### Questions about Others:

If more distant relatives or friends or charities are to be included, name each.

The mail address of every person and institution to be named in the will should be shown on your roster. All names should be precise.

Some of the answers to these questions should be supported by documents kept in a safe place. (See "Where Lodge Your Will?" found in Chapter 1, page 15.) Under varying circumstances, immediately after death it may be important to find one or more of the following: (1) military discharge papers; (2) deed to family cemetery plot; (3) certificate showing membership in a lodge; (4) marriage certificate (perhaps it is framed and on a wall!); (5) if a divorce was obtained in a distant county, a copy of final decree; (6) document attesting naturalization; (7) social security card; (8) testator's birth or baptismal certificate.

## ANTICIPATING THE OFFICIAL APPRAISALS

Valuations for tax purposes are first fixed as of day of death. In some jurisdictions there is an official appraiser appointed either by the court or the state taxing authorities. In others, valuations are reached by negotiations between the personal representatives of decedent and

IRS. There is an optional valuation date six months later. As to some assets, there can be little doubt. *The Wall Street Journal* will tell the story for listed and many over-the-counter securities. It may be easy to evaluate an urban residence.

In contrast, business ventures and, indeed, certain physical properties — real and personal — may be hard to appraise. Any owner may tend to have inflated ideas as to the value of the property. Here one wants no more than fair market value as the base for tax computations. So the postmortem planner should mellow any suggestions regarding value.

Suppose, for example, testator has valuable original paintings or other *objets d'art*. The proud owner has insured them at the maximum coverage available, actually considerably more than market value. The least the owner can do by way of helping the executor avoid excess taxes is to include with the other papers a realistic, down-to-earth appraisal by a recognized dealer or other expert, based on what *he* would pay, not what some eager collector might pay him.

I once saw a variance of 5 to 1 in respect to the appraisal of a picture. The "5" needless to remark, was that of the taxing authorities. Had the executor been armed with a rational appraisal, the state's appraiser might not have embarked on such a tangent. When reminded that the picture had been bequeathed to the art museum and a high valuation would not result in greater death dues, a compromise was quickly reached. But had the picture been bequeathed to a son or daughter, a minimum of $4,000 in taxes would have been at hazard; much more, if the bequest were to a distant relative or stranger to the blood. It is not fanciful to suggest that if the owner of an *objet d'art* has reached three score and ten, a realistic appraisal becomes more important than insurance coverage above true market value.

A fairly frequent appraisal problem, and a more important one in terms of dollars, comes with a business enterprise, whether it be testator's principal business or a venture outside his or her main occupation. Here often, if not usually, a buyout agreement is indicated. The enterprise itself, or perhaps the other stockholders or venturers (partners), will purchase a decedent's interest at an agreed price and terms. Perhaps the arrangement can be funded, or at least partially so, by life insurance. A most important caveat is this: Review and revalue at least annually; put the new valuation in writing; have all sign and have each keep a copy.

I represented the widow of a partner who died a few years after the end of World War II. During the dark days of the early 1930s, decedent and his associate agreed upon a fair buyout formula based on the then value of the business. Good friends and loyal partners, they overlooked adjusting price to reflect enormous equities built up after 1939. The widow is comfortable, but not wealthy. The surviving partner is rich. A good attorney will adapt an agreement to your needs.

## LIQUIDITY

In the course of drawing the will, testator and counsel will have estimated death dues. If the total estate, including life insurance, of an unmarried person is less than, say, $60,000, or that of married testators does not exceed $120,000, it is likely that they will disregard taxes, except for the marital deduction where applicable. As the estate mounts much higher, probable taxes, state and federal, should be computed and plans made as to the source of funds with which to pay them.

Life insurance, readily salable securities, savings accounts, and buy-out contracts are all familiar and natural assets which provide liquidity. If liquidity may be a problem, gifts of stock in a close corporation to reduce the taxable estate should be balanced against possible loss of a tax-free redemption, described shortly. Too large a gift might bring testator's stock below the required percentages.

There is another investment, not so well known. Certain issues of United States bonds are accepted at par for estate taxes regardless of current market or what decedent paid for them. The interest rate is not high; hence the bonds can usually be bought at a substantial discount, at 85 or even down to 75. One approaching death because of age or illness should consider buying enough to pay federal taxes. If, happily, the medical prognosis is wrong and testator lives a long time, the bonds will be paying interest. Posit federal taxes of $50,000 and bonds at 80. Enough bonds to pay the tax will cost $40,000. With no risk, a sure profit of $10,000, less death dues on this amount.

The bonds must be owned by decedent. So in a common law state, if the wife has separate property, she should buy the bonds to pay the taxes on her own estate, and the husband should buy the bonds to pay the taxes on his estate. In a community property state, they should buy double the estimated federal tax. After the first death, the unused half may be sold or held for the second death.

A prudent planner who travels abroad or faces an appreciable risk of being taken suddenly to the hospital in a terminal condition should consider the strategy of issuing a power of attorney to one or more suitable persons with full authority to each to buy the desired number of bonds in testator's name and stead, and in testator's name and on his or her behalf to borrow the required funds, pledging the bonds as security. It will be astonishing if testator's bank does not quickly respond affirmatively, closing the entire transaction within the hour.

There seems to be a general impression to the effect that federal death dues descend upon an estate sooner than they do. Taxes do not have to be paid within a few days or weeks of death. True, the traditional fifteen months within which the return had to be filed and taxes paid have been shrunk to nine. But still, IRS may grant a reasonable extension of time — six months' limit — for filing the federal estate tax return. Similarly, upon a showing of reasonable cause, the time for paying the federal tax may be extended until one year after a decedent's death.

The federal time schedule was shortened in 1970. Some states have already followed suit; it is expectable that all or most of them will.

IRS is not niggardly in granting extensions in time sufficient to take care of a short-term liquidity crisis. As a practical matter, it is seldom that a long-term liquidity problem is acute (unproductive "land-poor" property excepted) unless the estate consists largely of an interest in a wholly owned or a closely held business. The word "largely" as just used means 35 percent of the value of the gross estate or 50 percent of the taxable estate.

Perhaps the estate cannot raise funds with which to pay federal taxes without somehow liquidating stock held in the wholly owned or closely held corporations. A redemption of some or all of decedent's stock by the corporation would be the best way. But under ordinary rules, the money paid the executor for the stock would be considered as ordinary income, and so taxed. An exception is made for estates which meet a required formula. This gives an estate an opportunity to channel the value of the stock from the corporate coffers into the payment of estate taxes.

And in these circumstances, the executor may elect to pay part or all of the federal estate tax in two or more, but not exceeding ten, equal annual installments. Interest at the rate of 9 percent!

Hence I suggest that, while certainly testator should consider adequate liquidity as a major postmortem goal, the dilemma is not so desperate as is sometimes advertised.

You have already been alerted: If life insurance is made payable to a life insurance trust, the trustee should be instructed to lend funds to the executor if required for payment of death dues, federal or state, or income taxes owed by decedent.

# SUGGESTIONS AND ADVICE

In Chapter 9 under the subheading "Very Personal" (page 278), you were reminded of personal matters which must have attention within hours of death. In the preponderance of the cases, these arrangements are made by members of the family. The executor does not participate importantly unless he or she be within the family.

But if members of the family will not be on hand and are incapable of carrying on, the executor should be informed in advance, in detail, outside the will if it is not left in the custody of executor.

An executor should also appreciate, and the estate should benefit, from testator's ideas and advice concerning management and liquidation of properties. If testator possesses assets of substantial value of such a nature that specialized advice is needed, his or her suggestions may well include the nomination of experts: "C. D." for the machine shop; "E. F." for the two patents; and so on. And how handle the sale of the cabin cruiser or yawl?

Name personnel who may prove veritable Rocks of Gibraltar during the inevitable period of stress.

## FEES OF EXECUTOR AND COUNSEL

In states not hamstrung by an antediluvian statutory "commission" formula, there are two basic philosophies in respect to computing the fees of the executor and counsel. They are (1) on a percentage basis, and (2) on the fair value of services rendered, computed in respect to each estate. Proponents of a percentage basis will say that a percentage fee schedule charged by the executor bank or suggested in a so-called Advisory Fee Schedule of the Bar Association will average out and yield no more than a fair return to those who do the work. An answer is that each estate should pay its own proper bills. The compact, easy-to-process estate of one who has wisely planned and arranged his or her affairs should not be "averaged out" with a confused estate which requires an inordinate amount of time and talent during the period of postmortem management. Let me illustrate.

Some time ago, death took two valued friends and clients within a year of each other. The older had retired from active affairs. Despairing of either of his sons becoming a competent businessman, he disposed of his going manufactory. He also sold or, with an eye on tax benefits, gave away what he inaccurately termed "odds and ends," including his home. The house — turn-of-the-century vintage, built for a family with servants and horses — could not be sold at anywhere near its real worth. He gave it, one-fifth each year, to a nearby school which long had been looking toward it with yearning eyes. His investment portfolio was reduced to about twenty-five issues; still too many, the investment adviser said, but additional sales would have generated prohibitive capital gains. All stock certificates and bonds were neatly arranged in his strongbox. He left ample information, conveniently available.

Well prior to passing he made fee agreements with the prospective executor bank and with his attorney. The latter was already briefed; for several years they had worked together on the liquidation program.

Testator's prognosis was: a large but exceedingly easy estate. No appraisal problems. No responsibility in respect to selling or liquidating a going business. Assets all marketable. No minors, incompetents, or neurotics with whom one must deal. Postmortem management would be ministerial with no great problems with which to wrestle. An extraordinarily low percentage rate resulted in a modest round-sum fee which paid the executor bank and the counsel very well on an hourly basis.

In value, the other estate was about one-sixth the size. The principal asset was a retail store featuring style apparel for women. As the owner put it: "My inventory is always worth less than I paid for it. An item does not become valuable until some woman decides it was made for her."

Conscious of his coming demise, this testator did his best to sell, but fate did not grant him time. He did leave detailed recommendations as to how to carry on until the business could be sold.

Postmortem management of that smaller estate took at least ten times as many working hours as did the larger estate. Neither estate should be charged at a percentage rate deemed applicable to the "average" estate, whatever that word may mean.

So, having done an exemplary job of planning for postmortem management, the sick or truly senior citizen should go to his or her prospective executor and counsel, show them what has been done already, and make a fair arrangement as to the charges for the estate, in the absence of litigation or other event not then foreseen. If the fee amounts to more than testator thinks it should, careful inquiry may be made. Letters of confirmation from prospective executor and counsel will be a comfort to testator.

Some states persist with a long outmoded system of "commissions" fixed by law. If you reside in such a state, seek the guidance of a reputable attorney who deserves your confidence, and make the best arrangements the law permits.

## TWELVE

# The Nature and Measure of the Taxes

Death dues (duties) are of two breeds, estate taxes and inheritance taxes. The federal tax is an estate tax; it is measured by the aggregate value of the taxable estate transferred by death. It is not concerned with how much a particular beneficiary receives or his or her relationship to decedent. Its name reflects its nature — the United States estate tax. A dozen states also impose an estate tax.

Usually, but not always, the federal tax is by far the heavier of the two impositions. The observations made here regarding taxes will flow from the United States estate tax, unless a state inheritance tax is specifically mentioned.

# INHERITANCE TAXES

Except for Nevada, well financed by the gamblers, all states amerce some death dues. If an inheritance tax, it is imposed on the beneficiary, usually computed at an ascending scale as amounts increase, the rates graded according to the relationship of beneficiary to testator. A sampling of states illustrates the pattern.

| Relationship | Exemption | Tax Rate |
|---|---|---|
| Class A<br>Spouse lineal ancestor, lineal descendant | $5,000 to $25,000, some higher for widow | 1% to 10% |
| Class B<br>Brothers and sisters | $1,000 to $10,000 | 2% to 20% |
| Class C<br>All others | None | 10% to 30% |

When property passes to a Class A beneficiary, the inheritance tax is not a heavy burden. But when a large legacy falls within Class C or even Class B, the result may be onerous.

A thoughtful testator will usually direct that inheritance taxes upon specific bequests be charged against the residuary estate. A deduction from a monetary bequest or a payment of inheritance taxes by a beneficiary in order to receive the loved heirloom somehow makes the gift seem less gracious. The value of the bequest may be adjusted downward by testator if he or she thinks the tax might be an undue burden on the residuary estate.

As with gifts to charities, when a specific bequest is large in relation to the whole estate, a percentage limitation should be considered. "I bequeath unto Kathy the lesser of $10,000 or 10 percent of my estate after payment of taxes and expenses."

The impact of state taxes in the state of your domicile upon your probable estate must be explained to you by your own tax adviser, familiar with the tax laws of your state. He must be told the relationship to you of every legatee under your will. As shown in the preceding tabulation, if a legacy is to go to your spouse or child, the rate may be 1 percent; if to a cousin, it may reach 30 percent. When discussing inheritance taxes, your adviser may reinforce the admonition already given: Do not inadvertently slip into a position where a plausible argument can be made to effect that you are a resident of two or more states.

When planning the provisions of a wise will in respect to distributions and postmortem management, the affluent testator should inquire as to the possible impact of four other taxes and the possibility of savings: federal income tax; federal (now merged) gift tax; state income tax; and state gift tax.

Again, as illustrated in the preceding inheritance tax tabulation, factors other than size go into the calculation of death dues. But the ever-present, overriding ingredient is the size of decedent's taxable estate when valued in dollars.

# ESTATE TAXES

Internal revenue personnel should not be blamed too much for the exasperating procedures. The ascertainment of the dollar amount of death dues follows paths fixed by the terrain — that is, the reality that Congress has imposed taxes to be measured by value of assets. Unless the tax be amerced on the basis of gross assets (unacceptably unjust), there must be rules which guide the taxpayer and the taxgatherer as they reduce the gross estate to what is aptly termed "the taxable estate."

The United States Estate Tax Return (Form 706) was revised in 1972. Further revisions are doubtlessly now under way to conform to the Tax Reform Act of 1976. However, I think it is a safe assumption that the fundamentals of the prescribed returns will not be changed so as to affect their usefulness as illustrations in the discussions which follow. This is so because of the logic of the computation of a tax. It has and must continue to have three major aspects:

(1)  the scheduling and appraisal of gross assets;
(2)  the listing of allowable deductions; and
(3)  the computation of the tax based on the taxable estate, which is (1) minus (2).

The importance of an annotated inventory is stressed in Chapter 11 (page 173). A listing of assets which follows the United States Estate Tax Return is set forth there. So you have already read how IRS classifies your gross estate. Schedules A through I (page 174) are real estate, stocks and bonds, mortgages, notes, and cash or equivalent, life and other insurance, jointly owned property, other miscellaneous property, gifts which must be reported, powers of appointment, and annuities.

In some states, these assets are first appraised by persons appointed by the probate court or by the state taxing authorities. In others, the executor chooses appraisers who, he hopes, will be trusted by IRS. In some states the first step is the submission by the executor (personal representative) of his or her own appraisal of the value of the properties of the estate. All of these valuations are subject to adjustment by the Federal and State Taxing Authorities, and, in extreme cases, the courts.

The gross estate having been ascertained by adding Schedules A through I (page 320), the journey down to the taxable estate begins. The second phase of the tax return shows allowable deductions. They are:

SCHEDULE J: *Various Expenses*

It may be permissible and preferable taxwise to deduct some of the expenses of the terminal illness, funeral expenses and the expenses of administration when computing the *income* taxes of the estate and decedent. The approach in a community property state will differ from that in a common law state.

SCHEDULE K: *Debts of Decedent and Mortgages and Liens*

These will largely be based on claims filed and allowed, except when there is a valid lien, such as a first mortgage, of record when no claim need be filed.

SCHEDULE L: *Net Losses during Administration*
Usually limited to uninsured casualty losses such as damages to property. Expenses are elsewhere deductible.

SCHEDULE M: *The Marital Deduction* (Elsewhere discussed.)

SCHEDULE N: *Charitable and Public Bequests* (Discussed under "Gifts to Charities".)

SCHEDULE O: *Credit for Foreign Death Taxes*

SCHEDULE P: *Credit on Tax for Prior Transfers*
If decedent has inherited property, the death occuring within ten years before or, in a few *unique* situations, two years after that of decedent, a tax credit is allowed.
On pages 317 - 320 appears the classification of your assets presently

required by the United States Estate Tax Return. From the total of these assets will be subtracted the allowable deductions just listed (Schedules J through P) and other proper charges against the estate. In a community property state only half of the aggregate of the community property belongs to the decedent and would be taxable. And, with a properly drawn will in any state, the marital deduction will put the taxpayer in as favorable a position as one in a community property state.

Here we say farewell to the $60,000 exemption accorded every estate and always a part of estate tax practice and vocabulary. It is time to turn to the new method of calculation prescribed by the Estate and Gift Tax Reform Act of 1976.

## THE TAX REFORM ACT OF 1976

For many years Congress (particularly the members of the House Ways and Means Committee, the Senate Finance Committee, and their staff specialists, and finally the Joint Conference Committee and its personnel) have been working on a comprehensive revision of the Internal Revenue Code. In 1947 the Treasury Department and the Bureau of Internal Revenue, since rechristened the Internal Revenue Service (IRS), published detailed proposals for the integration of Federal estate and gift taxes. With expectable political flair, their efforts were labeled "reform," carrying a pleasant connotation of fairness toward the taxpayer, not to be found in a mere "revision."

Rather sooner than generally expected, the Congress passed and on October 4, 1976, President Ford signed the "Estate and Gift Tax Reform Act of 1976." The concurrent "reforms" in respect to *income* taxes, individual and corporate, are not within the purview of the Estate and Gift Tax Reform Act. Whether income tax rates will rise or fall will depend on economic and political pressures. As in the past, *estate* tax rates will probably tend to be steady. One reason is that estate taxes aggregate but a minor portion of the entire federal budget and a change in scale cannot affect the habitual astronomical deficits very much. Nor is there a great impact on the economy when a relatively few bereaved families pay somewhat more or less in estate taxes. In contrast, when all people with income are required to pay more (or less) of it over to the government the whole economy may be sharply affected.

In a number of instances the provisions of the Gift and Estate Act can best be highlighted by contrasting them with the former law, substantially unchanged for a full generation. This is so because former law vernacular has become a part of the vocabulary of all who have been reading or working in the field of estate planning. The $30,000 exemption in respect to gifts and the $60,000 exemption from federal estate taxation have been accepted by the taxpayer as something almost immutable. Now both are gone.

In their stead we must accept and incorporate into estate thinking a unitary concept of gift and estate taxes. As will be shown shortly, the two are unified (merged) and in essence there now is one ascending rate, from the cradle to the grave. No longer can the astute planner point to gift taxes averaging out at about three-fourths of federal death duties, with opportunities for substantial savings by the fortunate few whose financial resources permit large gifts (preferably) well in advance of death. In contrast, the 1976 law imposes a unified tax rate schedule for gifts and for property which passes because of death. For most purposes the new act became effective January 1, 1977. The unification brought into being a single cumulative taxing formula which measures all taxable transfers of property. Effective rates range from 32% to 70% for cumulated taxable transfers.

## CREDITS REPLACE THE EXEMPTION

Formerly as has been already recited, an individual with a taxable estate not exceeding $60,000 paid no estate tax. If (i) a husband and wife lived in a community property state or (ii) if in a common law state they had made proper use of the marital deduction, the bite of estate taxes was not felt until the net taxable estate reached $120,000.

Now the unified federal amercement for both gifts and inheritance begins with the first dollar in excess of the $3,000 *exclusion* per annum (still allowed in respect to each donee) and builds up until lifetime gifts are augmented, replaced, by the final legacy triggered by death.

The prospective donor-testator must not be depressed by this new way of computing the final amounts. For most families who plan properly the totality of estate taxes will be less, increasingly less during each of the next five years, then will level off at a "bottom line" figure which is comfortable when compared with the former impositions. The following schedule illustrates the merged (gifts and death) totals less *credits* on the tax which replace the traditional $30,000 or $60,000 exemptions.

# NEW METHODS OF COMPUTATION

*During 1977*

After computation of the unified tax based on the aggregate of all taxable lifetime gifts and the taxable estate of the 1977 decedent, a tax credit of $30,000 will be allowed. This is the equivalent of an exemption of $120,667 — a substantial increase favoring the taxpayer.

*During 1978*

During 1978 the credit is upped to $34,000. In the parlance of the abandoned "exemption" formula, this matches a deduction of $134,000.

*During 1979*

For the calendar year 1979, the credit becomes $38,000 . . . an equivalent to an exemption of $147,333.

*During 1980*

This year sees the credit reach $42,500 which is the equal of an exemption of $161,563.

*Plateau Beginning January 1, 1981*

Finally, for 1981 and thereafter, the credit will be $47,000. Translated into the "exemption deduction" language of the past, this is the equivalent of $175,625.

So as to this aspect, the taxpayer may well believe that the 1976 Act is truly a "reform" act. Assets insulated from the estate tax will have increased from the traditional $60,000 to $175,625. Indeed the exemption jump seemed so startling that when the congressional conferees finally agreed on it, a New York newspaper heralded the good news with a bold headline:

"ESTATE-TAX EXEMPTION IS
TRIPLED TO ALMOST
$176,000 BY CONFEREES."

The beneficent effect of the increasing credit is illustrated in the not infrequent estate in the quarter million dollar range.

|  | Taxable Estate | Tax before Credit | Deduct Credit | Net Estate Tax Payable |
|---|---|---|---|---|
| 1977 | $250,000 | $70,800 | $30,000 | $40,800 |
| 1978 | 250,000 | 70,800 | 34,000 | 36,800 |
| 1979 | 250,000 | 70,800 | 38,000 | 32,800 |
| 1980 | 250,000 | 70,800 | 42,500 | 28,300 |
| 1981 | 250,000 | 70,800 | 47,000 | 23,800 |
| There-after | 250,000 | 70,800 | 47,000 | 23,800 |

The figures listed in the second column are usually called the "tentative" tax, i.e. the tax before deducting the credit. It is taken from a prescribed schedule which begins at 18% for amounts not exceeding $10,000, obviously $1,800 if the combined taxable gifts and estate should happen to round out at $10,000.

Then, in twenty steps, the tentative tax climbs with language like this:

"Over $10,000 but not over $20,000 . . . $1800 plus 20% of the excess over $10,000."

"Over $20,000 but not over $40,000 . . . $3800 plus 22% of the excess over $20,000."

The riser points continue — $40,000, $60,000, $80,000, $100,000, $150,000, $250,000, $500,000, $750,000, $1,000,000, $1,250,000, $1,500,000, $2,000,000, $2,500,000, $3,000,000, $3,500,000, $4,000,000, $4,500,000, ending with an apex of $2,550,800 plus 70% of the excess over $5,000,000.

[Special provisions apply to the gift and estate taxes of non-resident aliens owning property situated within the United States.]

## SUNDRY CHANGES UNDER 1976 ACT

Here follow briefest alerts in respect to procedural and substantive changes under the Tax Reform Act of 1976.

1. How large must your estate be before you are required to file a federal estate tax return? The state inheritance tax return, it will be recalled, will probably name a lower figure.

Under prior law the personal representative was obliged to file an estate tax return whenever the gross estate of a citizen or resident was in excess of $60,000. For a death occurring during 1977, the minimum is $120,000. If during 1978, the minimum is $134,000. If during 1979, $147,000. If 1980, $161,000. If during 1981 or thereafter, $175,000.

If there have been taxable gifts subsequent to December 31, 1976 the minimum may be reduced. Competent advice should be sought before deciding not to file.

The new law (and regulations of IRS when they appear) must be consulted in respect to charging of expenses, including the cost of selling assets. Is an item deductible when computing taxes upon the estate or permissibly deductible when computing taxes measured by income? The latitude is not as great as formerly. The same charge cannot be deducted on both returns. Special mention will be made in respect to alertness to possible savings in the course of post-mortem management.

## CARRY-OVER VALUATIONS

For capital gain calculations on the pertinent income tax later imposed, beneficiaries will lose the much cherished stepped-up basis when the time comes to sell inherited property. By "stepped-up basis" is here meant the appraised value of property in decedent's estate which he may have bought long ago, at a low price, thus realizing a large capital gain.

The act provides that the beneficiaries' basis will be the same as the decedent's basis immediately before his death. However, for purposes of determining gain, basis will be "deemed" to be the fair market value of the property on December 31, 1976 plus death dues paid on appreciation since that date.

The appreciated value of property on December 31, 1976 is irrelevant to clarification of the deemed value because the IRS has a mechanical formula which ratably prorates all appreciation from the date of acquisition to the date of death.

The personal representative (executor) without special expertise will surely need advice from lawyers or accountants or both if the estate wishes results in these areas. It must be remembered that the truly small or moderate estate will not be burdened by excessive estate taxes.

# VALUATION OF FARMS AND FAMILY ENTERPRISES

The value of property for fixing estate and inheritance taxes is its fair market value. One common way of defining "fair market value" is to say it is the price a prospective buyer able and willing, but not under compulsion to buy, will pay an owner willing but not compelled to sell.

This definition necessitates contemplation of "highest and best use." For decades the Jones farm has yielded an income sufficient to support the family happy in their rural way of life. Recently suburbia has been approaching. The appraisers in grandfather's estate took the position that the "highest and best use" of the 320 acre farm would be a housing development, possibly with a mini-market area where the roads cross. This valuation was far above the appraisal by the county assessor for farm properties. Under the 1976 law, if prescribed conditions are met, the executor may elect to value the farm on a basis of its current use rather than on a basis of its "highest and best use."

Eventually when sold and subdivided for a housing project, there will be a great capital gain. But the estate taxes may be kept level.

Real estate incident to a closely held business may also qualify for valuation at present use. The act includes a dollar limit. The present use valuation can be used to decrease gross estates up to $500,000.

In order to receive the benefit of the new law with respect to these valuations,

a. The deceased must have been a citizen or resident of the United States,

b. The property at its highest and best use value must be greater than 50% of the gross estate,

c. It must pass to a qualified heir and must have been used as a farm or small business for five (5) of the last eight (8) years,

d. It must continue to be so used for fifteen (15) years after death.

There are additional requirements and numerous technical requirements and procedures which must be followed. Here clearly you will need the services of an expert.

Indeed, no principal is required for the first five years; the full amount is then payable over the next ten. Up to $1,000,000 the interest on deferred payments is presently set at 4%. Here is another instance where the 1976 Act works a "reform" favoring the taxpayer.

It is a comfort to know that under the new law, upon written request IRS must furnish a rather detailed statement explaining how it reached the valuations it proposes to use when determining estate taxes. The basis on which worth was determined must be supplemented by the computations used in reaching values. The IRS must also furnish a copy of written appraisals, if any, made by or for its use. Thus the taxpayer will be armed for appeals within IRS procedures or in court.

## INSTALLMENT PAYMENTS

The new law is beneficent in respect to stretching out payments. Having shown "reasonable cause" as best they can, the personal representatives of the estate may be able to extend payment of estate taxes on farms and closely held business properties over a fifteen year period. Earlier law allowed for an extension of ten years upon showing of "undue hardship" — a stricter test than "reasonable" cause. A ten year extension on an even lesser showing may be available.

The 1976 law contains formulas doubtless to be amplified by IRS regulations, in respect to what is required to qualify for extension benefits. (i) The closely held business in question must exceed 35%, and in some cases even 65%, of the value of the gross estate, (ii) or half of the taxable estate, (iii) the term "interest in a closely held business," means an interest and ownership as sole proprietor, or (iv) an interest as a partner in a partnership having not more than ten partners, or in which decedent owned 20% or more of the capital, (v) or ownership of stock in a corporation having not more than ten shareholders, or, as before, in which the decedent owned 20% or more of the voting stock.

It must be remembered that the new law will be followed by departmental regulations which will take years to evolve. Concurrently there will be court decisions, sometimes upsetting the regulations and ruling of the Internal Revenue Service. So for a long time there will be differences of opinion and uncertainty in response to the application of the Reform Act to particular situations. Indeed, cases are still pending in court as to the meaning of the old act, superseded on October 4, 1976.

## COMMUNITY PROPERTY OWNERSHIPS

Obviously the character of property — separate property vis-à-vis community property — becomes significant when considering what the will should say and what the death dues will probably be.

The community property formula is so easy to comprehend that I will define it before looking at the preponderant common law ownerships. The moment before death, the community property spouses own their property together, each having one indivisible half. The wife does not own four dining-room chairs and the husband four. Each owns half of all, half of each molecule, atom, and neutron, carried as far down as the physicist can imagine.

After death, the survivor *continues to own* his or her half; it cannot be reached by decedent's will. Suppose that their community assets net $500,000. One-half remains with the survivor. Decedent's estate is $250,000. Confident that it will be passed on to their children, decedent wills his or her community half to the surviving spouse. On the second death, the estate will be in the order of $450,000 depending upon the investment acumen and thrift of the survivor.

Americans are mobile; many are affluent, modern gypsies. What if Sam and Sue lived in a common law state and then in a community property state? Or vice versa? Or, living first in common law Vermont, they move to community property California, and then, after ten years on the Pacific, Sam is promoted to Chicago. At the time of the first move, a policy regarding future ownership should be determined and suitable records maintained. The fundamental rules will aid testator in this important planning.

1. A change of domicile does not of itself affect the nature of property which had already been acquired by the spouses at the time of the change of domicile.

2. It follows that property which is separate property under the law of the state wherein it was acquired remains separate property if the spouses move to a community property state. The income from that property is separate property unless mingled with the community funds of the spouses.

3. Community savings continue to be owned one-half each if the spouses move to a common law state. Again if kept segregated, the income of the transported community savings belongs to the husband or to the wife as the case may be.

Revocable trusts may be convenient mechanisms to segregate common law and community assets, and prevent commingling if not desired.

A potential bride in a community property state who expects to walk down the aisle to marry a man of means, and has even slight reason to believe that community earnings will be nil or nominal and that they will live on his investment income, should consider the advisability of an antenuptial agreement. (Chapter 8, page 226) Otherwise, upon her husband's death she might find herself with (1) no community property, (2) no more than a token in his will, and (3) no dower rights.

## COMMON LAW OWNERSHIPS

It will not be profitable to step back from the 20th Century and tell of the former harsh concepts of property rights as between husband and wife. He was the sovereign as between them and usually became the virtual owner of her property. The position of the wife in respect to property has been ameliorated, state by state, by legislation sometimes given as a generic term — The Married Women's Acts.

Property rights as between husband and wife are determined by the laws of the state in which the spouses reside or, perhaps, have resided. Local counsel must be consulted as to ownerships, prerogatives of dower and all other inter-husband and wife worldly relationships.

Since, with variations favoring the wife, the forty-two common law states still follow the basic common law concept that the earnings of the husband and the savings therefrom belong to him, she is not apt to own very much, unless she inherits wealth, is a big earner on her own or has emerged the winner in a large divorce settlement ending a previous marriage.

The big, taxable estate is usually that of the husband, in sharp contrast with a community property state where the entire estate stemming from their joint efforts, or the product of either, during marriage is owned equally.

Because under either system of marital ownership, either spouse may own separate property from other sources, careful study may be required before reaching a conclusion as to how taxes can best be minimized.

## THIRTEEN

# On Saving Taxes and Expenses

Despite literature seemingly to the contrary, the objective should not be to save the last penny in taxes. The target should be to save every tax dollar which can be saved without significantly distorting the wisest plan for your estate and family. Sometimes it is better to forego tax savings which, after debate, were deliberately permitted by the Congress.

Deliberate *evasion* of taxes lawfully due is wrong and may be criminal. Note that I did not say "justly" due. A tax is imposed by a legislative body anxious for income, not by a court seeking justice. This stern reality leads naturally to the rule that

369

taxpayers may minimize their taxes as much as they lawfully can within the framework of the laws imposing the taxes. There is nothing opprobrious about *avoiding* taxes whenever the law permits. If the legislators and taxgatherers have left open a socially undesirable "loophole" (to use a popular political term), it is up to them to plug it. Meanwhile, the taxpayer may use it.

Indeed, during 1970 the Massachusetts court approved a tax-avoidance gift program from the property of a person not mentally competent to decide whether to give away her property. The ward was an elderly lady. Her estate was in the $1,200,000 range; annual income exceeded $50,000. The conservator (the guardian) was her daughter, herself with two daughters and four grandchildren. Contrary to a guardian's traditional duty to conserve the ward's estate and to take nothing from it, the conservator petitioned the probate court for permission to give:

1. To herself $30,000 plus $3,000; total $33,000.
2. To each of conservator's two

daughters and four grandchildren, the sum of $3,000; total $18,000.

The grand total was $51,000 — carrying with it a prophecy of further gifts of $21,000 a year as long as the ward should live.

The avowed purpose was to take advantage of the then $30,000 lifetime exemption and the $3,000 still available annual exclusion from federal gift taxes. A Massachusetts statute specifically authorizes a guardian to apply excess funds toward the establishment of an estate plan to minimize taxes or to give to the ward's natural beneficiaries.

The Supreme Judicial Court of Massachusetts upheld the conservator as she drew on the estate of her incompetent mother for the benefit of herself, her children, and her grandchildren when the laudable objective was to save federal taxes. This decision by a preeminent court is among many which sanctify your efforts to minimize taxes.

# THE MARITAL DEDUCTION

Only the residents of the eight community property states (see Glossary) could see justice in a system of federal taxation under which in Iowa, for example, the estate of husband and wife who had managed to save $200,000 would be taxed about $31,500 on the death of the husband, while in Nevada the tax would be about $4,800. The vast majority of voters resident in common law states could not be convinced by the minority in the eight community property jurisdictions that the legal ownership by the wife of half of the couple's savings entitled them to this special tax advantage. So in 1948 Congress authorized the marital deduction.

As then enacted, the essence was that a husband might pass to his wife (or the wife to her husband) up to a maximum of one-half his or her adjusted gross estate tax-free. One may not say simply "one-half the estate" because, in the fashion of those who conceive tax legislation, the allowable deduction is reached by formula. Prior to working on particulars with the laywer, it

372

was sufficient for the married estate planner to remember: "If I give up to about one-half direct to my spouse, I take that much off the top of my estate. My now merged gift and estate taxes should dive." The immediate net federal effect was to raise the nontaxable estate of two married persons to $120,000.

Yet a testator might elect not to accord to the spouse the freedoms of ownership which accompany a gift by way of a marital deduction. He may prefer that his estate pay the higher tax. Here is but one instance.

At age sixty-six, a year after he retired as president of his company, a wealthy man becomes a widower. He had two children, both in comfortable but modest circumstances. He and his wife had planned on ten or fifteen years of travel. What would now happen to his travel plans? A comely widow, aged forty-two, took care of that. They were married.

It was a happy marriage. Home for the best weather, they followed the birds and spent a full fifteen years visiting and revisiting the utmost parts of the earth. As of the day of his last will, his two children were still comfortable but not prosperous; grandchildren were at various stages of schooling and getting started in business. His wife's one child, a son by her first marriage, was in the line of promotion at Sears.

Testator's wife was now approaching fifty-eight, but he felt that if his death should occur within the next few years, she would remarry. From his own happy second experience beginning at age sixty-seven, he would want her to.

By using the maximum marital deduction, federal estate taxes on his death would be about $50,000 less than if he established a single residuary trust to protect his second wife and his children — one which would certainly pass to his own two children and their issue after her death. The marital deduction formula is inconsistent with certainty that the principal will some day reach testator's own descendants. The Internal Revenue Code requires that the surviving wife have freedom to will (to appoint) her share to whomever she pleases. Should testator risk having a large portion of his fortune diverted to (1) his wife's affluent son by her first marriage, or (2) her third husband or his progeny?

Testator elected to control the estate which he had built up during forty-five years of effort. He provided for his second wife with allowances most generous. But, after her death, his fortune would return to his own bloodstream. Cost: *circa* $50,000 in taxes levied against his estate at high rates. "Worth it," he grumbled.

The act and IRS regulations permit the gift to be in trust. Many wills therefore have at least two trusts: (1) the marital deduction trust, and (2) the residuary trust. The latter may be routed as testator desires after the second or subsequent deaths. (As will be seen, the 1976 act sharply curtails generation skipping.) The corpus of the marital deduction trust must be subject to testamentary disposition by the surviving husband or wife and be reachable by creditors.

Not having been taxed on the first death, the assets of the marital trust are of course taxable in the estate of the surviving spouse, but at beginning rates.

The critical marker is that the spouse to whom the gift is made must have full rights to his or her share, including the power to designate beneficiaries. Testators have been prompted to put strings on marital bequests through fear that the widow or widower will remarry and the estate be diverted from their own children. Such a restriction vitiates the marital deduction and the property is taxed at top rates in the first estate.

When available and properly used, the marital deduction is preeminent among tax-saving opportunities.

The 1976 Act enlarges the range of marital deduction. First, as to gifts: Either spouse may give to the other up to $100,000 free of gift tax. The second $100,000 is taxable. Half of marital gifts over $200,000 is taxable and half is tax free, i.e. after $200,000 a 50% maximum marital deduction is allowed plus, of course, the $3,000 annual exclusion.

Turning again to the impact of death on the new marital deduction tax formula: The optimum estate tax marital deduction is the greater of $250,000 or one-half of the decedent's estate. Suppose John Doe dies subsequent to January, 1977, leaving an estate of $300,000. He has elected to make the maximum marital deduction of $250,000 leaving an adjusted taxable estate of $50,000.

Using a much larger estate as the alternate illustration: The decedent husband's taxable estate was about $1,000,000. He elected the marital gift route for a full half of it. His taxable estate deflates to $500,000. The estate tax on $1,000,000 should have approximated $345,800; with the marital half to his wife, the estate tax would be $155,800, a saving of $190,000!

As already stated, the price testator paid for this great gift to his wife was the risk that *his* hard earned savings might reach unacceptable alien coffers.

## ON SAVING TAXES AND EXPENSES

In some aspects the Tax Reform Act of 1976 makes it more difficult to program substantial savings.

A most natural way to reduce the estate is for testator to make lifetime gifts to the very people who will be beneficiaries under the will. A law imposing an estate tax requires an accompanying law imposing a gift tax. Without it, many estates would be reduced to minuscule size by *inter vivos* gifts to testator's loved ones. So the Congress has long imposed a *gift* tax upon the donor. Now, as you have read, this gift tax is now merged into the unified estate tax.

It has been seen that both federal and state taxes are based on the appraised value of the gross estate, less allowable deductions, resulting in the taxable estate. The unpleasant end-result is that the maximum savings in death dues cannot be obtained unless you are willing to reduce the dollar value of your taxable estate. Though painful, it is not legally difficult to minimize or even eliminate death duties. All one needs to do is to renounce wealth; become a Buddhist with naught but a beggar's bowl! Whether that would reflect wisdom is an entirely different question. For the mystics and others who abjure things worldly, "Yes." For most of us, there is no problem; relatively few families face prohibitive gift and estate tax brackets.

We now turn to channels through which the taxable estate may be reduced in a fashion, which it is hoped, is not inconsistent with testator's desires.

## GIFTS TO PEOPLE

Here is where the Tax Reform Act of 1976 hurts. The unified tax has taken away the opportunity of making large gifts to loved ones at three-fourths the estate tax amercement plus the advantage of removing the income from the corpus of the gift from the top income tax bracket of the donor and eliminating the principal given away from the estate of the donor-testator. Now, as has been emphasized, the gift and estate tax rates have been merged. They ascend one ladder.

But savings, lesser but worthwhile, are still possible. The $3,000 annual exclusion remains. The count is by donees, not a total of the aggregate given by the donor.

This time the illustrative family consists of grandfather, grandmother, three children and six grandchildren. Not a preposterous family by most planned parenthood standards.

Grandfather may give $3,000 a year to each child and a like sum to his or her spouse — $18,000 to the three couples plus $3,000 to each grandchild, again a total of $18,000 — a grand total from granddaddy of $36,000. Grandmother may do the same. From the two of them, $72,000. For the "modestly rich" that is not trivial, particularly if pursued as an annual program as long as health and resources permit. Rounding it out at $70,000 a year for but five years, $350,000 has been taken from the top brackets of the grandparents' estate plus the tax advantage of less income on which to pay income taxes at highest applicable rates.

Here comes a factor which plays into the hands of the tax-gatherer: It is the natural human tendency toward procrastination. Most parents, grandparents, uncles, aunts and other potential benefactors "have been thinking about it" for a long time before they do it. I venture the unprovable assertion that *most* people who give relatives or friends up to $3,000 per annum could have started the program much sooner.

If a *well situated* senior generation begins a $3,000 per year beneficiary gift program as soon as it *safely* can, the estate tax may be reduced far more than a person might guess. I have deliberately over-emphasized. "Well situated" and "safely" are both in italics! It is not sound family and social policy for the elders to reduce their own assets below a clearly safe margin to draw upon if later years should prove expensive.

Obviously I have assumed a steady family, loyal and cooperative. For reasons which seem good and sufficient, the affluent present generations may not want to put unrestricted funds within the power of their own children, much less their grandchildren not yet through the prodigal son stage of life.

The 1976 Act tightens the rules in respect to gifts in contemplation of death. Formerly a gift within three years of the demise was presumed to be in contemplation of death. But the representatives of the estate were given an opportunity to prove that the gift was motivated by compelling "life" purposes. Now all gifts beyond $3,000 per donee made during the three years immediately preceding the passing are includable in decedent's estate.

## ON SKIPPING GENERATIONS

The term "generation-skipping" defines itself. It is exemplified in the typical situation where wealthy grandparents (first generation) have affluent children (second generation) who possess children of their own (third generation). Occasionally, the generations have already marched on and the third-generation grandchildren, themselves well-situated financially, have children, the fourth generation.

Affluent first-generation testators should weigh the possible desirability of leapfrogging one or even two generations, depending on the circumstances and personalities involved. Second-generation testators may well do the same. There seems to be a widespread impression that all possible estate tax benefits resulting from "generation-skipping" have been eliminated by the 1976 Act. That is not so. The field is not as free as before the Act. The previous practically limitless possibilities have been curtailed. A generation-skipping tax has been devised. The Treasury Department is given authority to prescribe rules. Nevertheless, worthwhile opportunities remain which are adequate for most families.

This is so because the Act includes an exception of $250,000 per child of the testator. It is a trifle confusing. The exclusion from tax is measured by the number of persons in the second generation when the benefit runs to the third generation, i.e. the grandchild.

The $250,000 exclusion allocated to their parent will be divided between the grandchildren.

Restating: The grandparents have, say, three children. The exclusion of $250,000 per child to the mandate against generation skipping applies $250,000 each to these three progeny, but not to their progeny. How much each grandchild will benefit depends upon the number of grandchildren in that line of descent. One grandchild without brothers and sisters would benefit three times as much as his cousins, three in one family.

Another illustration: John and Mary (typically, but not necessarily, grandparents) can transfer up to $500,000 in trust with a life time interest in their two children, Ivan and Gretchen, without a tax being imposed upon the termination of the children's interest in the trust. Validation of the assets for these purposes is made at the time of passage to the third generation.

The inhibitions against generation-skipping-transfers are effective for trusts or similar legal devices created subsequent to April 30, 1976. The new provision is not applicable to trusts that were irrevocable on April 30, 1976, or, in the case of a decedent dying before January 1, 1982, pursuant to a will or revocable trust that was in existence on

April 30, 1976 but was not amended at any time after that date in regard to generation-skipping transfers.

## GIFTS TO CHARITIES

The tax incentives to charitable gifts have been retained.

It has already been shown that there is a multiple benefit in giving to charities during one's lifetime. Assume a $2,000 gift to a church meets IRS requirements for deduction from taxes measured by income. The triple tax benefits are:

   i. Year of gift, $2,000 less upon which to pay income taxes.
   ii. Each succeeding year, $120 less (at 6 percent) to report for income taxes.
   iii. On death, $2,000 less in estate.

Statutory percentages limit largess to charities when deducting gifts for the purpose of computing taxes measured by income. With death dues, the rule is different. If testator devised and bequeathed everything to qualified charities, there would be no tax.

1. *Bequests Direct to Charities:* No

problem need here be indexed if testator mandates distribution from the estate direct to the charity or to a charitable trust for the sole benefit of the charity except: (a) testator must be sure each charity is qualified under IRS regulations; and (b) when making a testamentary bequest, a percentage limitation should be included as cautioned in Chapter 3 (page 72).

2. *Charitable Remainder Trusts:* In its ordinary sense, the word "remainder" of course means what is left or what remains. In law, it is an ownership which takes effect after another estate is terminated. Thus: All of the income of trust shall go to my wife as long as she lives. Upon her death the then principal of the trust and accumulations shall be distributed to the Children's Hospital. The testator has created a charitable remainder.

Prior to 1969 such a natural bequest sequence created no problem. The estate tax was computed on the value of the wife's interest in the trust based on her life exceptancy. The remainder going to the charity was not taxed.

As was observed in Chapter 3, page 73, shrewd people took advantage of the opportunity to shift principal to income (to the wife, away from the charity). At the behest of IRS, Congress passed severe restrictions in respect to charitable remainders. New terms, such as "Unitrust," "Annuity Trust," and "Pooled Income Fund," have been coined.

Charitable remainder trusts are also used when making gifts to charities during one's lifetime. Using a Unitrust as the example: Donor *ir*revocably transfers funds or property to a trustee or direct to the charity, his alma mater. The trust requires that he (perhaps also his wife) be paid an income for life, typically 5 percent of the fair market value of the assets as valued each year. Donor-testator may make worthwhile savings in income taxes as well as reduce the size of the estate against which death dues will be amerced.

This emphasis on the marital deduction and gifts to persons and charities as the principal routes to a reduced estate and therefore to lower death dues is not intended to exclude other avenues. When the estate is of great magnitude, ingenious tax experts — legal and accounting — can sometimes suggest adjustments of holdings within the family and other special measures which will result in important savings. As one example: In unique situations, a massive estate may be channeled into multiple trusts (one for each of a dozen beneficiaries!), thus saving on *income* taxes, if testator's instructions are such that capital gains and other income taxes, or part of them, will be taxed against the trust estates. The price is less flexibility in providing for the changing needs of beneficiaries, as well as possible increased costs of administration.

## REPORTING OF GIFTS

Prior to January 1, 1977 a gift tax return was required for each calendar quarter during which a donor made a gift valued in excess of the annual *exclusion* of $3,000 attributed to each donee. Charitable transfers were similarly reportable. The new law is less onerous. The *quarterly* filing is demanded only when:

(1) Taxable gifts made during that calendar year, plus,

(2) All other taxable gifts made during that calendar for which a return was not yet required exceed the sum of $25,000.

The annual filing day for gifts (not yet reported) which exceed $3,000 but during the year did not reach $25,000 is the succeeding February 15.

## U.S. BONDS ACCEPTED AT PAR

Money will be saved and funds provided for the payment of federal taxes if testator holds one or more of the issues of United States bonds acceptable at par for the payment of estate taxes. That desirable program was reviewed as part of liquidity planning (Chapter 11, page 329). The new law imposes a capital gain tax upon the difference between the cost (or value December 31, 1976 if then held) and the face value.

# BY POSTMORTEM MANAGEMENT

The business acumen of the executor may make a big difference in the value of the distributable estate, that is, in the part that reaches the beneficiaries. Particularly when there are to be substantial distributions in cash in contrast with divisions in kind among beneficiaries, the executor should not ignore the market value of the portfolio or even of trends in the value of real estate. Suppose, as of the day of death, the testator owned ten different stocks of a total value of $100,000, plus enough cash in banks to pay all expenses. A bachelor, he named five beneficiaries, bequeathing one-fifth of his estate to each. If his executor decides to retain all the securities and distribute one-fifth of each to each beneficiary, serious complaint of mismanagement will be unlikely even though the market price drops during the months between death and distribution. A beneficiary will receive exactly what he or she has been willed.

Suppose, in contrast, that the beneficiaries include a flock of nephews and nieces, all living in Hungary. As a practical matter, the securities must be sold and distribution made in cash. If prior to sale the market booms, the executor is applauded as wise. If values drop, he may be accused of mismanagement. If prudent, he will have secured a written analysis of the portfolio and recommendations in respect to sales from an investment adviser of impeccable repute. If real estate should be sold, the viewpoint of a skilled appraiser should leaven the salesmanship of the real estate broker.

An alert executor may liquidate frozen assets of the deceased for twice as much as would someone of meager competence. But, except when the decision hinges on the commonsense business judgment of the executor, the tax savings resulting from astute postmortem management may be dependent upon technical expertise. Occasions for tax savings include:

1. *Alternative Valuation Date.* Choosing between the alternative valuation dates

would seem simple enough. The Internal Revenue Code permits an election between the date of death and six months thereafter. The value of land does not often fluctuate violently and visibly within half a year. So it is not unnatural for an executor to check market or available trading valuations of the securities in the portfolio and elect the lower total. But it is not quite so arithmetical as that. An illustration *up* and an illustration *down* will suffice. *Down.* Suppose the principal asset of the estate to be the former family farm, recently opened as a lakeside residential subdivision. It is convenient to a huge factory. Lots were selling fast; houses were going up. A few weeks after death, almost without warning, the plant cut back to a skeleton crew. Sales of lots ceased. Repossessions commenced. Rental signs appeared. Six months after death, owner's true equity in the subdivision was anyone's guess. It was mortgaged to finance streets, sewers, and utilities.

IRS recognized the unusual

predicament of the estate and reduced valuations to a bearable amount.

*Up.* The executor did not do so well. The value of the aggregate estate approached $500,000. All but about $60,000 was represented by stock of the family corporation. On day of death, decedent's portfolio of publicly held stock was worth about $35,000. During the six months after death, the stock market plummeted. Decedent's list lost $4,700 with the market.

Aware of the market, the executor elected the alternative date six months after death. But he overlooked the primary asset, the stock in the family corporation, none of which had ever been sold. He failed to examine the corporate books to ascertain operating results during the past half-year. The death of the founder had not hurt the corporate shadow which lived after him. Never had the company made so much money. IRS gladly accepted the alternative date, lowering the value of the listed investment portfolio by $4,700 and increasing the value of the close corporation by nearly $70,000.

2. *Relative Income Tax Brackets.* The assets of the estate yield considerable income. The principal beneficiaries of the estate are in high income tax brackets. A savings may come from the retention of income in the estate. Or, in contrast, not having yet received their inheritances, the beneficiaries are in low income tax brackets. Then the executor may save taxes by distributing income received by the estate, thus putting the flow of income into a lower rate structure.

3. *Allocation of Expenses.* Alternatives are available in respect to the allocation of the costs of administration, principally the fees of the executor, the appraisers, accountants, attorneys, and court costs. Should they be deducted on the United States Estate Tax Return *or* when submitting the estate's income tax return? Perhaps medical expenditures incident to the last illness may be advantageously allocated as claims either against decedent's final income tax return or against the estate.

4. *An Accumulation Trust.* In Chapter 5 (page 120), an accumulation trust was defined and was suggested as a tool in building flexibility into your estate plan. The tax aspects are complex and, seemingly, everchanging. But alert postmortem managers may make adjustments in the flow of money which will result in substantial savings in taxes.

5. *Choosing the Tax Year; Timing of Distributions.* Choosing the best tax year, both for the estate and for the trust which follows after, may involve business judgment as well as the columnar work sheets of the accountant and the cautious prognosis of the lawyer. Should the fiscal year be fixed in anticipation of heavy losses during the coming spring and summer? Closely related is the date of distribution; here the financial interests of beneficiaries may differ. The executor must proceed with an even hand.

6. *Previously Taxed Property.* The executor must not overlook the possibility of a credit for previously

taxed property. If an asset became a part of the estate within the preceding ten years because of a death, and taxes were paid, there is a tax credit usable when computing taxes on the second death. If the two deaths are but a year or so apart, the credit is considerable. Then it dwindles down and, by the end of the decade, it disappears.

7. *Joint Income Tax Returns*. IRS permits an executor to file a joint income tax return with the surviving spouse. (That is, if he or she has not remarried prior to the end of the taxable year!) Lower rates may result.

These are, I believe, among the most frequent occasions available to postmortem managers for tax savings. But there are others, some rare.

For example, it may be to the dollar advantage of the family as a whole if a prosperous legatee refuses to accept (disclaims, renounces) the designated bequest. Or if a wealthy donee renounces a power of appointment. Tax burdens are shifted to the clansmen who are in the lowest brackets. The 1976 Act prescribes definite rules in respect to disclaimers.

And then there are situations where a surviving spouse may elect to stand by his or her statutory rights rather than take under the will. Usually these are highly technical procedures, depending on the law of the state wherein the parties dwell.

This capsule discussion of tax savings through intelligent management might well have been included in Chapter 6 to illuminate the importance of choosing executors and executrixes skilled in estate matters or, if the potential tax savings may be significant, instructing your inexperienced nominee to retain the best technicians available. Tax savings by alert management are of course possible after subsequent deaths as well as after the first death.

# FOURTEEN

# Save Your Advisers' Time

The noun "advisers" in the title of this chapter is in the plural. Testator may, and, if the will is to include one or more trusts, usually should, seek the advice of trust officers. (Not an infrequent or improper front for comparative shopping as testator is deciding, "Which bank shall I use?") Testator's competitive life underwriters will prepare schedules and submit recommendations — usually to buy more insurance. Even at the early planning stage, a large estate may have an accountant. He may accompany his schedules with sagacious suggestions, but the bulk of his time is spent with sheets of paper at his accustomed hourly charge, and there is little you can do about it except to have kept your records straight. Unless you take out more insurance, the salesman will cost you nothing. Neither will the trust officers unless you establish an *inter vivos* trust. The one place where you can save considerable charged-for time is the law office.

Not much legal time is either justified or, in fact, usually consumed when the estate is modest in size and the will simple.

All to my wife and if she should predecease me to the University Congregational Church.

This type of will may require no more of the lawyer than a ten-minute chat with the client and brief dictation to a secretary, plus formalities of signing. Were it not for the rigid rituals in regard to execution, a "do-it-yourself" job, following a form, would seem safe enough.

In sharp contrast, an involved situation may require the lawyer to spend many days: interstate and tax aspects, desirability of *inter vivos* gifts, trusts, probable valuations, and, perchance, the best way of handling some family troubles that are better left unmentioned in any document.

The purpose of this short concluding chapter is (1) again to emphasize that relatively large savings in postmortem costs will usually result from adherence to the precepts of Chapter 11, and (2) to stress that *you can yourself keep down the cost of developing your estate plan and completing the implementing will.*

Your attorney will be handicapped in helping you evolve the structure of your estate unless you promptly and fully inform (brief) your counsel in respect to the big "W"s.

1. What?
2. To Whom and When?
3. Why?

It is the function of the law to have mechanisms available for the accomplishment of every feasible, lawful purpose. I believe it has. If you provide adequate information in respect to the four "W"s, the burden is upon the lawyer to find a legal way and to phrase the very best "How" for whatever you wish to achieve.

The conscientious attorney will attempt to become fully informed regarding "What," "To Whom and When," and "Why." But sometimes (I could certainly say "often," and by stretching it a little, perhaps "usually") it is a time-consuming procedure — which must be charged against the client.

There is no purpose here to suggest duplication of the data gathering so earnestly recommended in Chapter 11. If, prior to your first trip to the lawyer's office, you have already prepared an inventory with explanatory notes and the personal information data, take copies along. They will supply the necessary answers to all, or at least most of your attorney's questions regarding the first two "W"s — "What" and "To Whom." If you have not yet prepared a complete list of your assets, no matter. You will have in hand a reminder memo so that you can tell the approximate totals in each category of assets and your obligations. That is all the lawyer needs to know at this stage about your property, and perhaps it is as much as you wish anyone to know during your lifetime.

After the outline of the inventory (page 322), Chapter 11 catalogs the data personal to testator, spouse, children, and other beneficiaries which must be available to the executor. Here, a wife, thinking of her will, might respond, "My husband is executor. He already knows all these things." But what if the husband passes first, or simultaneously in a common accident? The bank as successor executor and the attorney will waste their expensive time searching for data and documents easy for testator and testatrix to gather in advance.

For drawing of the will, counsel may not need all the detail which will be required by the executor. But testator's time will be saved if he or she gathers the suggested personal information and uses it for a dual purpose — to assist the lawyer in the drawing of the will and the executor in postmortem management.

Again, as in the inventory, if the personal data compilation is not done before your first visit with counsel, have with you a memo of those items which you believe pertinent to the *drawing* of the will in contrast to administration.

If you are considering a trust, have in mind your tentative viewpoint in respect to the limit on drafts to meet emergencies, a marital trust, sprinkling, accumulations, power of appointment, your distribution formula both as to income and principal, provisions pointed to beneficaries with special problems, and so on. And of course: Who shall be trustee?

In Chapter 3, beneficiaries were grouped into (1) preferential beneficiaries, (2) primary beneficiaries (spouse, children, grandchildren, and stepchildren), (3) secondary beneficiaries, and (4) tertiary beneficiaries. Approaches and formulas were suggested. But in some respects your estate and its beneficiaries may be unique. The frequently used patterns would not attain the end-result which you desire. For you, without any unfairness to anyone, one of the beneficiaries whom I have classed as secondary or even tertiary may be in fact the primary beneficiary. For sound reasons, acceptable to all toward whom you owe a duty, the conventional, the expectable primary beneficiary might be limited to a token bequest, plus a few words indicating why.

Perhaps testator is one of the multitude who finds a chart or an outline a help in thinking things through to a conclusion. If so, in supplementing the roster, have ready for the lawyer an outline of testamentary objectives somewhat as follows:

### OUTLINE OF OBJECTIVES

1. PRIMARY BENEFICIARIES: Here note who comes first, and to what extent. Differentiate between principal and income. State which assets (whether

realty, intangible investments, or things) pass directly to primary beneficiaries with no restrictions, or go for life only, or are to be in a trust under which he or she is first beneficiary.

2. SECONDARY BENEFICIARIES: Here note your wishes regarding those who come next. If your estate should be less in value than you expect, rationing may become essential. It is the prerogative of testator to name the priorities and percentages.

3. TERTIARY BENEFICIARIES: A modest bequest to the Boy Scouts might be listed with the primary beneficiaries. But if your will speaks in terms of buying land and constructing a camp, the tertiary beneficiary percentage concept considered in Chapter 3 (page 70) will apply.

So, in your attorney's hands as you begin to discuss what your will should say, will be:

1. Your annotated inventory, or a summary giving totals according to nature of asset; sufficient personal data

2. An earmarking of assets which will not pass under the will

3. An approximation of your obligations, classed as secured and unsecured

4. The roster of people and institutions under the will plus those (children or spouse) who must be named even though there is no inheritance

5. The outline of your objectives as to each class of beneficiary

You have, as the English put it, "briefed" your solicitor. You are not having the professional, at your expense, dig for data which you yourself can bring in. Even more important, I think, than the dollar saving in lawyer's time will be the better job you both will be able to do for your estate and its beneficiaries. You will write a wiser will.

Since a principal purpose of a will is to

give the testator peace of mind, your wishes are of controlling importance. If counsel believes them impractical or unwise, he will tell you. Some attorneys may disagree with some of the suggestions of this book. In your situation, your counsel may be quite right and have something better to offer. As to substance, the determination is yours. As to the technicalities, the tax impacts, and the wording, the lawyer will have the expertise.

In deference to those with relatively small estates and blessed with an uncomplicated family, I must again remark that I realize the procedures recommended in Chapter 10 pertaining to conserving time and expense *after* you are gone, and the suggestions of this chapter concerning saving your lawyer's time as you work on your will, may seem complicated and unnecessary. In many instances you will be 100 percent correct. But, I think, for most there will be at least a few applicable and useful suggestions.

This discussion opened with a quotation — a definition of "will" — from the first edition of the revered *Encyclopaedia Britannica*. It is fitting to close with a bit of wisdom from the 200th Anniversary Edition.

> In the United States a will tends to be lengthy and complicated, and it appears unwise ever to draft one without expert legal advice.

The *Britannica* editors also admonish that

> in order to keep up not only with the changing circumstances of testator's family circle and his property but also to keep abreast of the frequent changes in the tax laws and thus to avoid unnecessary taxes, it is advisable for a testator to have his will regularly checked.

When the size and complexities of the estate justify, the legal advice recommended by the Society of Gentlemen in Scotland may be expanded to include one or more of the ancillary advisers — trust officer, accountant, insurance expert, or investment counsel. Thus may your estate plan be made plain, as simple as is possible, fair, and workable, with expenses and taxes kept to a minimum. Even when in most elemental form, covering minimal assets, your will should not be entirely a do-it-myself project. But each final decision must be yours and the final draft should be exactly as you want it.

# Glossary

**Abatement**: A proportional diminution of legacies when the assets available to pay them are not sufficient to pay them in full.

**Ademption**: The act of a testator who, during his lifetime, (1) pays to a legatee the sum which was to pass to him later under the will; (2) gives the legatee the object which the will bequeaths to him; or (3) parts with the subject of the bequest (e.g., a car), thus making the bequest inoperative.

**Administrator**: A man or institution appointed by the court to administer the estate of a person who died without a will (i.e., intestate). **Administratrix**: A woman so appointed. **Administrator (trix) with the will annexed**: The person or institution appointed by the court to carry out the terms of a will which lacks an executor. See **ancillary.**

**Ambulatory**: Revocable; subject to change.

**Amerce**: To impose a tax or fine. **Amercement**: The pecuniary penalty.

**Ancillary**: Auxiliary to or attendant upon. **Ancillary administration**: Proceedings in a state other than that wherein the principal probate case pends brought to clear title to property in the foreign state.

**Annuity**: A periodic payment of a sum certain in money for life or for a designated term.

**Attestation**: The act of witnessing the execution (signing) of an instrument and subscribing it as a witness.

**Attorney-in-fact**: See **Power of attorney**.

**Beneficiary**: One for whose benefit a trust is created. One to whom a bequest is made.

**Bequeath**: To transfer ownership of personal property by will, resulting in a **bequest** (a legacy).

**Caveat**: Beware. Let the doer beware.

**Charitable**: Herein used broadly to include all religious, educational, health, character-building, and other eleemosynary activities.

**Close corporation**: A corporation the stock of which is held by very few persons, who are usually also the officers of the company.

**Codicil**: A supplement adding to, deleting, or modifying the provisions of a will. Executed with the formalities of a will, it may be admitted to probate.

**Common law**: Loosely, as distinguished from other systems of law and from statutory enactments, rules of action deriving authority from usage and court decisions.

**Community property**: Property deriving from the efforts of either husband or wife during marriage and hence owned in common in a sort of marital partnership. Recognized in Arizona, California, Idaho, Louisiana, Nevada, New Mexico, Texas, and Washington.

**Consanguinity**: Kinship; the relationship of persons descended from a common ancestor.

**Contingent**: Dependent upon some future uncertain event, such as a **contingent beneficiary**, who is a beneficiary only when surviving someone else.

**Corpus**: The principal of an estate or trust.

**Curtesy**: The right a surviving husband may have in the estate of his deceased wife.

**Custodian**: One who has custody; a guardian, a keeper, a trustee.

**Decease**: Death; to die. **Deceased, decedent**: A dead person.

**Descent and distribution**: The division of the property of intestates among those legally entitled thereto.

**Devise**: A disposition of realty by will. **Devisee**: The person to whom realty is given by will. **Devisor**: The person who transfers realty by will.

**Distribution**: Commonly applied to the distribution of property, real and personal, whether under a will or an intestacy.
**Distributee**: See **descent and distribution**.

**Domicile:** That place where a person has his or her permanent home, in contrast to a temporary residence, of which one may have several. Betokens of domicile are where the person (1) proclaims her or his home to be, (2) votes, (3) lists her or his address on important papers, (4) conducts business transactions, (5) joins clubs, (6) has bank accounts, and (7) is listed in directories.

**Donor:** One who makes a gift. **Donnee:** The person who receives a gift.

**Dower:** The provision which, in many states, the law makes for a widow out of the property of her husband for her support and the nurture of their children. **Dowager:** A widow so endowed.

**Election:** The right a spouse may have to take under the will or, alternately, under the laws of intestacy.

**Eleemosynary:** See **charitable**.

**Escheat**: A reversion of property to the state for want of any individual in line to inherit.

**Estate**: The interest or ownership which anyone has in property, real or personal. See **future interest; life estate.**

**Ex parte**: Done on the application of one party only, without the need of notice to any person (if any there be) adversely interested.

**Execution**: The signing of an instrument. The performance of a contract. Carrying out of the terms of a will.

**Executor**: A man or institution appointed by a testator in his or her will to carry out the terms of that will. **Executrix**: A woman so appointed.

**Extremis**: Sick or injured beyond hope of recovery, and near death. Such a person is *in extremis*.

**Fee simple:** Unqualified ownership; clear of any condition, limitation, or restriction.

**Fiduciary:** A person invested with rights and powers to be exercised for the benefit of another, to whom the fiduciary owes scrupulous good faith, candor, and meticulous honesty.

**Future interest:** A potential ownership which cannot be enjoyed until some future time.

**Guardian:** One who has the legal care and control of the person or property, or both, of a minor or an adult who is incompetent.

**Heir:** The person appointed by law to succeed to an estate in case of intestacy.

**Holograph:** A document written *entirely* by the hand of the person who executes it. **Holographic will:** A will totally handwritten.

**Intangible property or intangibles:** Evidences of ownership or debt, such as stock certificates, bonds, promissory notes, contracts, and franchises.

**Inter vivos:** Made during one's lifetime. (Literally, between living persons.)

**Interest:** Any right in the nature of property. Usually used when the ownership is less than all or absolute. A partial or undivided right; title to a portion.

**Intestate:** Without a valid will. **Intestacy:** Dying without a valid will.

**Irrevocable:** Cannot be revoked. For example, an irrevocable trust.

**Issue:** Offspring. A descendant or descendants.

**Joint tenancy (ant):** See **tenancy; tenant**

**Jurisdiction:** The range of judicial or

administrative authority; herein used as the equivalent of a state.

**Laissez faire**: The principle of noninterference by government with the action of individuals.

**Legacy**: A gift of personal property made by will; a bequest. **Legatee**: One who receives a legacy; distributee.

**Letters of administration**: A certificate issued by the court showing that the administrator named therein has qualified and is authorized to administer the estate.

**Letters testamentary**: The instrument issued by the probate court to an executor or executrix empowering him or her to discharge the duties of this office.

**Life estate or interest**: An ownership limited to the life of the owner or, rarely, of some other named person.

**Lineal descent**: Direct line of descent,

as from father to son to grandson.

**Marital deduction**: A deduction allowed when computing federal estate taxes and the decedent spouse has willed up to roughly one-half the estate to the surviving spouse.

**Marital trust**: A trust which meets the requirements of the Internal Revenue Code permitting either spouse to give roughly half his or her property to the other without imposition of estate taxes. Such property is taxable on the second death.

**Marshaling assets**: The arrangement of claims so as to secure the proper application of the assets to the various claims.

**Ministerial**: That which is done under the authority of a superior or the flow of a system; that which demands obedience to rules, but requires no especial discretion or judgment. **Ministerial act**: One which a person performs in a prescribed manner in obedience to legal mandate or tradition, without basal exercise of his or her own judgment.

**Per capita:** Dividing an estate by giving an equal share to each designated person. Compare: **per stirpes.**

**Perpetuity:** Literally, unlimited time. The rule against perpetuity forbids a restriction which defers complete and unrestricted ownership for a period beyond life or lives in being, plus twenty-one years plus such periods of gestation as in fact exist.

**Per stirpes:** That mode of reckoning the shares of descendants whereby the children of any one descendant divide only the portion which their parent would have taken if living. Compare: **per capita.**

**Personal property, personalty:** Movable property, tangible and intangible, chattels; anything not real estate.

**Personal representative:** Executor (trix) or administrator (trix). Sometimes used in a broader sense.

**Personalty:** See **personal property.**

**Posthumous child:** Born after the death of the father or, when a Caesarean section is performed, after that of the mother.

**Pour-over will:** A will which directs that all, or a portion of, testator's estate flow into an already-existing or independently established (as life insurance) trust.

**Power of appointment:** An authority conferred by will or other proper instrument upon a person (the "donee") to determine who is to receive property or its income after the termination of named interests. **Limited power:** For example, a husband's will gives his wife power to appoint which of their children and their issue is (are) to receive his trust estate after her death. **General power:** No limitation upon authority of donee.

**Power of attorney**: A writing by which a person constitutes another as his attorney (often called "attorney-in-fact") to act in his place.

**Primogeniture**: Seniority by birth in the same family.

**Probate**: Strictly: the process of proving a will to be genuine. Customarily: the legal and bureaucratic process which takes place after a person dies, enabling his or her representatives to pass on his or her property to the heirs. **Probate asset or estate**: Property which passes under one's will in contrast to that which does not, such as (usually) life insurance and joint tenancies and accounts with the right of survivorship. **Probate court**: The court in which probate proceedings are heard; also called "surrogate," "orphans," "chancery" court or "court of ordinary." **Probate proceedings**: The processes (notices, petitions, hearings, and orders) whereby the law is applied to the several subjects within probate jurisdiction, including the administration of estates of decedents, whether or not there be a will; appointment of guardians and supervisors of the properties of minors and incompetents; sometimes, trusts.

**Pro bono publico**: For the public good.

**Prudent man rule**: A rule for those holding funds of others; these persons are expected to make investments with regard to expected income as well as the probable safety of the capital to be invested.

**Real, realty**: Pertaining to land and the fixed improvements and, usually, the growing things thereon, as contrasted with personal property (personalty) which is movable and may be intangible.

**Remainder**: An estate (ownership) which takes effect after another estate has terminated. **Remainderman**: One who is to receive the trust property after the rights of the prior beneficiary have ended. Compare: **reversion.**

**Residuary:** Pertaining to the residue. **Residuary legatee:** One who receives the residue of an estate.

**Residue:** The portion of an estate remaining after payment of claims, expenses, and taxes, and distribution of whatever has been specifically devised and bequeathed.

**Reversion:** That part of an ownership which is not disposed of and returns (reverts) to the grantor or his or her successors when the lesser intermediate estate ends. Compare: **remainder.**

**Revocable:** Subject to being revoked, as a revocable trust.

**Spouse:** Either husband or wife.

**Sprinkling:** A power given to a trustee to use its discretion when making allocations or distributions among two or more beneficiaries. (Colloquial.)

**Surrogate**: A person appointed to act for another. In some states, the judicial officer handling probate matters and guardianships.

**Tenancy**: A holding of land by any title of ownership. **Tenancy in common**: The ownership of fractional interests by two or more persons in the same property. **Joint tenancy with right of survivorship**: On decease of a joint tenant, the entire tenancy remains in the survivors, and at length in the sole survivor.

**Tenant**: In every day usage, the opposite of "landlord"; the property is not the tenant's own but belongs to another person with whose consent the tenant occupies it. In law, every possessor of property is a tenant. **Joint tenant**: Variously, tenancy in common or joint tenancy with right of survivorship.

**Testamentary**: Pertaining to a will. Effective upon the death of the maker.

**Testamentary capacity**: Able to understand the nature of a will and the consequence of making it. **Testamentary disposition**: Direction of the disposition of property by will or codicil or by a trust made in contemplation of death or not to take effect until death.

**Testate**: Having a will. **Testator**: A person who makes a will. **Testatrix**: A woman who makes a will.

**Tort**: Accidental or deliberate injury to person(s) or property.

**Trust**: The holding of property, real or personal, for the benefit of those for whom the trust was created, usually persons or institutions other than the trustor, but occasionally the trustor in a dual capacity as beneficiary. An *inter vivos* trust is established during the lifetime of trustor, the person who creates it. **Testamentary trust**: A trust established by will. **Charitable or public trusts**: Trusts designed for the benefit of a charitable institution or the public generally, rather than named individuals and their successors. **Contingent trust:** Trust that depends for its operation upon a future event.

**Trustee:** The person or institution designated by the trustor or appointed by the court to administer a trust.

**Trustor:** The creator of a trust. Sometimes **donor**, grantor, settlor, or founder.

**Usufruct:** The right to use profits and proceeds of property, perhaps owned by another.

# INDEX*

*Note: See also Glossary for definitions.

437

The publishers hope that this Large Print Book has brought you pleasurable reading. Each title is designed to make the text as easy to see as possible. If you wish a complete list of the Large Print Books we have published, ask at your local library or write directly to:

G. K. Hall & Co.
70 Lincoln St.
Boston, Mass. 02111